SPAD XIII
VS
FOKKER D VII

Western Front 1918

JON GUTTMAN

First published in Great Britain in 2009 by Osprey Publishing,
Midland House, West Way, Botley, Oxford OX2 0PH, UK
443 Park Avenue South, New York, NY 10016, USA

E-mail: info@ospreypublishing.com

A CIP catalogue record for this book is available from the British Library.

Print ISBN 978 1 84603 432 9
PDF e-book ISBN 978 1 84603 876 1

Edited by Tony Holmes
Cover artwork, cockpit and armament scrap views by Jim Laurier
Three-views by Harry Dempsey
Battlescene by Mark Postlethwaite
Page layout by Ken Vail Graphic Design, Cambridge, UK
Index by Michael Forder
Typeset in ITC Conduit and Adobe Garamond
Maps by bounford.com
Originated by PDQ Digital Media Solutions, Suffolk, UK
Printed in China through Bookbuilders

09 10 11 12 13   10 9 8 7 6 5 4 3 2 1

FOR A CATALOGUE OF ALL BOOKS PUBLISHED BY OSPREY MILITARY AND
AVIATION PLEASE CONTACT:

NORTH AMERICA
Osprey Direct, c/o Random House Distribution Center, 400 Hahn Road, Westminster, MD
21157
E-mail: uscustomerservice@ospreypublishing.com

ALL OTHER REGIONS
Osprey Direct, The Book Service Ltd, Distribution Centre, Colchester Road, Frating Green,
Colchester, Essex, CO7 7DW, UK
E-mail: customerservice@ospreypublishing.com

www.ospreypublishing.com

German ranks	French ranks	USAS ranks	RFC/RAF ranks
Rittmeister (Rittm)	Capt de Cavallerie	Cavalry Captain	Cavalry Captain
Hauptmann (Hptm)	Capitaine	Captain	Army Captain
Oberleutnant (Oblt)	Lieutenant	First Lieutenant	Lieutenant
Leutnant (Ltn)	Sous-Lieutenant	Second Lieutenant	Second Lieutenant
Offizierstellvertreter (OffzSt)	Adjutant	Warrant Officer	Warrant Officer
Feldwebel (Fw)	Sergent-Chef	Master Sergeant	Master Sergeant
Vizefeldwebel (Vzfw)	Maréchal-des-Logis	Sergeant 1st Class	Sergeant 1st Class
Sergeant	Sergent	Sergeant	Sergeant
Unteroffizier (Uffz)	Caporal	Corporal	Corporal
Gefreiter (Gfr)	Brigadier	Private 1st Class	Private 1st Class
Flieger (Flgr)	Soldat	Private	Private

Editor's Note

For ease of comparison between types, imperial
measurements are used almost exclusively throughout this
book. The exception is weapon calibres, which are given in
their official designation, whether metric or imperial.
The following data will help in converting the imperial
measurements to metric:

1 mile = 1.6km
1lb = 0.45kg
1 yard = 0.9m
1ft = 0.3m
1in. = 2.54cm/25.4mm
1 gal = 4.5 litres
1 ton (US) = 0.9 tonnes
1hp = 0.745kW

Acknowledgements

Thanks to Frank W. Bailey, Alex Imrie, Colin Owers,
Allan Toelle and Greg VanWyngarden for their assistance
during the preparation of this volume.

Cover Art

At 0900 hrs on 14 September 1918, Fokker D VIIs of
Jasta 18 ambushed SPAD XIIIs of the 13th Aero Sqn over
Thiaucourt, resulting in Ltn Hans Müller claiming three
aircraft destroyed and single victories being credited to
Ltns Günther von Büren and Heinz Küstner. One of the
Americans who survived this action was 1Lt Leighton
Brewer, and he subsequently recalled, 'On the 14th we
were given a low patrol, at a height of 2,500 metres. We
were flying this when we were attacked by a group of red-
nosed Fokkers. We lost four aeroplanes within one minute!
I was flying between a couple of men who were shot
down, but I only got one bullet in the tail of my
aeroplane. The first indication I had that enemy aircraft
were nearby was when I saw a red Fokker with a white
fuselage standing on its nose and spraying the fellow
behind me with bullets. Two Fokkers with red wings and
noses and white fuselages dived on us, and they shot down
the men on either side of me. 1Lts Charlie Drew, George
Kull, Buck Freeman and "Steve" Brody were all lost. Drew
was very badly wounded, Kull was killed and the other
two were captured'. 1Lt Charles W. Drew, who was later
to have his wounded leg amputated, was actually taken
prisoner. Two Fokkers were jointly credited to 1Lts Robert
H. Stiles, Gerald D. Stivers and Murray K. Guthrie, but
Jasta 18's only casualty was Ltn von Büren, who was
wounded. The 13th's veteran commander, Capt Charles J.
Biddle, ruefully attributed his losses to the fact that in
spite of his relentless warnings, 'the new men will get
carried away with themselves in a combat and go too
strong.' (Artwork by Jim Laurier)

CONTENTS

INTRODUCTION

If the Sopwith Camel and Fokker Dr I are universally regarded as the iconic dogfighting antagonists of World War I, the second most familiar pair – among Americans at least – is the SPAD XIII and the Fokker D VII. Each has its own claim to fame.

France's first twin-gun fighter, the SPAD XIII brought a 53rd, and final, victory and subsequent tragic death to France's most famous ace, Georges Guynemer. It also later served as the definitive mount for its most successful fighter pilot, René Fonck. As the principal fighter of the US Army Air Service (USAS), the SPAD XIII was the aeroplane in which its 'ace of aces', Edward V. Rickenbacker, and the top-scoring American balloon-buster Frank Luke each earned the Medal of Honor. Both France and the United States regard it as their chief instrument of victory in the skies above the Western Front in the conflict's last months.

Opposing the Allied fighters in the final stages of World War I was the superb Fokker D VII. Although it entered combat too late to be flown by Germany's leading ace Manfred Freiherr von Richthofen, the D VII was used to deadly effect by the second- and third-ranking German aces, Ernst Udet and Erich Löwenhardt. More importantly, it had the distinction of being regarded by its fliers and its foes alike as the best all-around fighter aeroplane of the conflict.

As is so often the case in history, the reality behind these classic images calls for some qualification. Far from being an absolute 'wonder aeroplane', the Fokker D VII could be outpaced by the SPAD XIII both in level flight and in a dive. On the other hand the D VII climbed faster, was more manoeuvrable at slower speeds and was reported by numerous Allied opponents to have the added trick of being able to 'hang on its propeller', peppering them from below with machine gun fire.

The robust airframes of both aeroplanes reflected the past three years' structural advances, the SPAD's being conventional 'wood and wire', but fundamentally sound

from inception, whereas the Fokker's incorporated a welded steel fuselage frame and an innovative wooden cantilever wing structure that eliminated the need for bracing wires as used on the SPAD, heralding monoplane designs to come.

Both aircraft had their shortcomings. The spur reduction gear employed to adjust the Hispano-Suiza 8B engine's 220hp to the SPAD XIII's most efficient propeller speed proved to be a perpetual malfunction waiting to happen, especially in its early months of use. Visibility from the cockpit, though excellent in the upper plane, was marred by some blind spots for which SPAD pilots had to vigilantly compensate when over enemy lines.

Poor ventilation within the Fokker D VII's cowling often caused its machine gun ammunition to ignite, with the nightmarish consequence of in-flight fire. Quality control at Anthony Fokker's factory at Schwerin had acquired a reputation for unreliability that also bred vigilance on the part of Germany's Inspektion de Flieger, or Idflieg for short. Ironically, better built D VIIs were produced under licence by Fokker's longtime rival, Albatros.

Sous-Lt René Paul Fonck of SPA103 was the most successful French SPAD XIII pilot, with nine documented victories over Fokker D VIIs among his total of 75 kills. His tunic covered in medals, Fonck is seen here posing proudly with his fighter in the spring of 1918. (Jon Guttman)

An early Fokker D VII caught climbing seems to embody the phenomenon of 'hanging on its propeller' that so many Allied pilots attributed to it. (Jon Guttman)

When they were functioning at full efficiency and being flown by competent pilots, there was little to choose between the SPAD XIII and Fokker D VII. By the time the latter appeared over the Western Front, however, the German Army was in a late stage of the offensive it had begun on 21 March 1918. Early on, there were barely enough D VIIs to replace the Dr Is as the vanguard of a fighter force still heavily dependent upon ageing Albatros D Vas and Pfalz D IIIas to offset a steadily growing number of first-rate Allied counterparts. Too few examples of the new Fokker fighter were available in the summer of 1918 to allow units equipped with the aircraft to achieve air superiority by the time the last German offensive failed on 18 July.

From then until the Armistice on 11 November 1918, the Germans remained on the defensive, just as they had been prior to March. This gave the Fokker pilots the same tactical advantage that their Albatros-flying colleagues had enjoyed the year

Ltn Ernst Udet, commander of Jasta 4 and Germany's second-ranking ace with 62 victories (including eight SPAD XIIIs), poses before a BMW-engined Fokker D VIIF that was marked *LO!* in honour of his fiancée, Lola Zink. (Greg VanWyngarden)

before, using methods already proven for achieving localised air superiority, aided by prevailing winds that favoured their side of the lines. Yet in spite of these inherent disadvantages, by August 1918 the SPAD pilots were encouraged to go on the offensive by the strategic initiative their armies possessed on the ground, along with superior numbers, stocks of fuel and a growing reservoir of trained, combat-experienced airmen.

September 1918 saw the launching of Allied offensives that achieved breakthroughs unimaginable even a year earlier. The British and Australians gained territory east of the Somme River and in Flanders, and the French took the Aisne River and liberated parts of the Champagne region. That month also saw the first large-scale pushes by the Americans, at Saint-Mihiel and in the Argonne Forest, which the Germans came to see as enough of a threat to deploy two of their most combat-seasoned fighter wings, or *Jagdgeschwader*, to the latter region. Consequently, the duels between SPAD XIIIs, which now fully equipped the USAS pursuit squadrons, and Fokker D VIIs reached a crescendo.

By that time the concept of air superiority, and the technology and techniques for achieving it, had been fully realised, and were being taken seriously. Although fighter pilots still strove for the fame of acedom by downing five or more enemy aeroplanes, the knightly game of single combat had given way to confrontations between flights, squadrons, groups or wings in what amounted to sprawling air battles. Aerial warfare had come of age, and in the final epic dogfights of World War I the SPAD XIII and Fokker D VII symbolised its state-of-the-art embodiment.

CHRONOLOGY

1916

10 May   Aviation Militaire places its first order for SPAD VIIs.

August   SPAD VIIs enter frontline service.

December   Seeking to improve SPAD performance, Hispano-Suiza develops high-compression 180hp 8Ab and larger 200hp reduction geared 8B engines.

1917

February   SPAD XIII, powered by Hispano-Suiza 8B engine, ordered into production.

April   First SPAD XIIIs arrive at the front for evaluation.

13 June   Capt Frederick Sowry of No. 19 Sqn RFC scores first SPAD XIII victory over a German two-seater. Lt G. S. Buck uses SPAD XIII to destroy an Albatros the next day, and Sowry drives an Albatros D III down out of control on 21 July.

20 August   Capt Georges Guynemer of Escadrille N3 uses newly delivered SPAD XIII S504 to shoot down a DFW C V over Poperinghe for his 53rd, and last, victory.

11 September   Guynemer killed in action in S504.

December   French units report 131 SPAD XIIIs in frontline service, but engine problems, mostly with the Hispano-Suiza 8B's spur reduction gear, are grounding them two days out of three.

1918

January   Fokker V11 and V18 win fighter competition at Adlershof, earning acceptance for production as the D VII.

Adversaries at rest – SPAD XIII S15561 No. 30 of the 94th Aero Sqn shares an unidentified airfield with a surrendered Fokker D VII shortly after the armistice. (Kenneth L. Porter Collection via Greg VanWyngarden)

21 March   Operation *Michael* begins the Kaiserschlacht, Germany's last bid for victory in the West.

Late April   First Fokker D VIIs arrive at JG I's Jasta 10.

9 May   Ltn Erich Löwenhardt of Jasta 10 credited with first Fokker D VII victory, an SE 5a, followed by a DH 9 the next evening.

27 May   Germans launch Operation *Blücher-Yorck* in the Aisne sector between Soissons and Reims. Ltn d R Rudolf Windisch, commander of Jasta 66, is brought down by Sous-Lt Souleau and M d L Cavieux of SPA76, his Fokker D VII falling into Allied hands.

29 May   Flying a Fokker D VII lent to him by JG I, Hptm Rudolf Berthold, CO of JG II, scores the type's first success over a SPAD XIII when he shoots down Sgt André Gelin of SPA77 south of Soissons.

14–20 July	Last German offensive of the war culminates in Second Battle of the Marne, which ends with Germans in retreat and French launching a counterattack across the river.
25 July	First victories by USAS SPAD XIIIs of the 95th Aero Sqn, including 39-victory ace Ltn Karl Menckhoff of Jasta 72, brought down by 1Lt Walter L. Avery and captured.
12–18 September	St Mihiel Offensive, the first American-commanded operation of the war. Fokker D VIIs of JG II inflict heavy losses on USAS, including SPAD XIIIs from the 1st, 2nd and 3rd Pursuit Groups.
14 September	Jasta 18 claims five SPAD XIIIs in one combat – three by Ltn Hans Müller – for the loss of Ltn Günther von Büren, wounded in action. The 13th Aero Sqn USAS loses four SPADs, with one pilot killed and three captured.
25 September	Capt Edward V. Rickenbacker of the 94th Aero Sqn downs an LVG and an escorting Fokker D VII in an action for which he will be awarded the Medal of Honor – in 1930.
26 September– 6 November	Allied Meuse-Argonne Offensive pits American and French SPAD XIIIs against Fokker D VIIs of JG I and JG II.
26 September	Lt René Fonck of SPA103 claims six German aircraft in one day for the second time in his career, including three Fokker D VIIs. Ltn Franz Büchner of Jasta 13 downs three SPAD XIIIs of the 1st Pursuit Group and a Salmson 2A2.
29 September	2Lt Frank Luke Jr of the 27th Aero Sqn burns three balloons, bringing his total to 14 (plus four aeroplanes), but is shot down and mortally wounded by anti-aircraft fire. Posthumously, he becomes the first USAS member awarded the Medal of Honor.
6 November	Fokker D VII pilots of JG I claim three SPAD XIIIs for the 'Flying Circus' last victories.
11 November	Armistice.

1919

28 June	Signing of Treaty of Versailles, which includes a specific clause demanding surrender of all Fokker D VIIs to Allies.

Capt Edward Rickenbacker (left) shares a photo opportunity with the trio of mechanics on who he depended to keep his Hispano-Suiza 8B engine functioning. (Greg VanWyngarden)

DESIGN AND DEVELOPMENT

SPAD XIII

When World War I broke out in the summer of 1914, military aviation was in its infancy and the concept of air superiority barely existed. By the end of 1916, the essential fighter configuration had been defined – a single-seater with a forward-firing machine gun, usually synchronised to fire through the propeller. For the rest of the conflict, aircraft manufacturers of the warring powers engaged in a constant struggle to gain an edge in speed, rate of climb or manoeuvrability that would give their side control of the sky.

One influential factor in that quest was the water-cooled eight-cylinder 150hp Hispano-Suiza 8Aa engine devised by Swiss engineer Marc Birkigt in 1915, around which several great Allied fighters were designed. The first such aircraft, however, was not so much designed for that powerplant as serendipitously adapted to make use of it.

Created by Louis Béchereau for the Société anonyme pour l'Aviation et ses derives, the SPAD SA series sought to provide forward-firing armament by placing a gunner in a pulpit held by means of struts in front of the propeller and its 80hp Le Rhône 9C rotary engine. Introduced in late 1915, the SA 1, SA 2 and SA 4 were more terrifying to their front gunners than to the enemy, but their basic airframe was sound. Therefore, on 4 June 1915, Béchereau applied for a patent for his designs' single-bay wing cellule, which featured intermediate struts of narrow chord, to which the bracing wires were attached at the midpoint. That arrangement added strength and, by reducing vibration in the wires, lessened drag as well.

Béchereau's next fighter, the SPAD SG, was essentially a single-seat SA 4 with a remotely controlled Hotchkiss machine gun in an unmanned nacelle in place of the pulpit. Evaluated in April 1916, it too was a failure, but then Béchereau altered the airframe to use the newly developed 140hp Hispano-Suiza 8A engine and armed it with a synchronised 0.303-in Vickers machine gun. Originally designated the SPAD SH, the prototype had a large conical spinner when test flown in March 1916. The spinner was abandoned but its rounded radiator shell was retained.

A further development known as the SPAD 5 used a 150hp 8Aa engine that reportedly gave it a maximum speed of 105mph and the ability to climb to an altitude of 9,840ft in nine minutes. An impressed Aviation Militaire ordered 268 fighters on 10 May 1916.

The final production model was officially designated the SPAD 7.C1 (the 'C1' indicating that it was a single-seat *chasseur*, or fighter), but was more widely known as the SPAD VII. Initial cooling problems were eventually solved after trying a number of different radiator configurations. The 3,500 SPAD VIIs that were eventually built served the air arms of – and were flown by aces from – France, Britain, Russia, Belgium, Italy and the United States. French fighter pilots were still training in SPAD VIIs as late as 1928.

The inevitable development of improved German fighters in the late summer of 1916, most notably the Albatros D II with its twin machine guns, led ranking French ace and zealous SPAD advocate Georges Guynemer to write to Béchereau in December calling for more power and heavier armament. Birkigt's interim solution was to increase the compression ratio of his original engine, resulting in the creation of the 180hp 8Ab, which kept the SPAD VII's performance competitive right up until the end of the war.

Meanwhile, on 11 June 1916, Hispano-Suiza had successfully bench-tested the new 8B engine, which generated 208hp at 2,000 rpm at ground level, and used a spur reduction gear to transfer that power to the propeller.

After testing the 8B in a SPAD VII, Béchereau concluded that a somewhat larger, more robust airframe would be required to accommodate it. In addition to its size, the

SPAD XIII S504 shortly after its delivery to SPA3 at St Pol-sur-Mer in August 1917. Capt Georges Guynemer would score his 53rd victory with the fighter on 22 August, and subsequently die in it on 11 September. (SHAA B97.1685)

SPAD 13.C1, which was ordered into production in February 1917, had rounded wingtips, inversely tapered ailerons, forward-staggered cabane struts with a frontal bracing wire and, most significantly, twin 0.303-in Vickers machine guns with 380 rounds each. A parallel development, the 12.Ca1, combined a 37mm Puteaux cannon with a single 0.303-in Vickers. And while it achieved small-scale production and enjoyed modest success when flown by some of France's aces, it proved to be such a handful to fly that aces were about the only pilots who could fly it.

Sous-Lt René Dorme, one of the many aces in Guynemer's escadrille N3, test-flew one of the new SPADs at Buc on 4 April 1917, and at least one was undergoing evaluation in a frontline unit on 26 April. The first aerial victory claim in a SPAD XIII, however, came from Britain's Royal Flying Corps (RFC), which had adopted the SPAD VII in the summer of 1916 and acquired SPAD XIII S498 in late May 1917. Given the British serial number B3479 and tested at Candas, it exceeded expectations with a speed of 140mph at 15,000ft, reaching that altitude in 16 minutes and 18 seconds.

On 9 June B3479 was sent to No. 19 Sqn for evaluation, and on the 13th future RFC ace Capt Frederick Sowry drove down a German two-seater for his third victory. Lt G. S. Buck destroyed an Albatros whilst flying it the next day, and on 21 July Fred Sowry drove an Albatros D III down out of control northeast of Ypres.

The first Frenchman to score in the SPAD XIII was Capt Guynemer who, flying S504 from St Pol-sur-Mer, near Dunkerque, shot down a DFW C V over Poperinghe on 20 August for his 53rd – and last – victory. On 11 September he and S504 failed to return from a mission. Later, a sergeant of the German 413th Regiment stated that he had witnessed the SPAD's crash and identified the ace's body, but an Allied artillery barrage drove the Germans off before they could bury him. Evidence suggests that Guynemer was the victim of Rumpler C IV crewmen Flg Georg Seibert and Lt d R Max Psaar of Fl Abt (A) 224w, who were themselves slain shortly after by Belgian Lt Maurice Medaets.

Adj Pierre Gaudermen (at far right) of SPA68 examines his aeroplane after a rough landing at Toul aerodrome during the winter of 1917–18. This view affords a good view of the rounded wing tips of the early-model SPAD XIIIs. (SHAA B76.623)

In addition to 20 pre-production machines, the Aviation Militaire ordered an initial production batch of 250 SPAD XIIIs, but by December 1917 only 131 had reached the front. The delay was primarily due to problems associated with the Hispano-Suiza 8B's reduction gear, which continued to handicap it for months thereafter.

In addition to that, reports came in of bulging fuel tanks, eventually remedied by a modified pressure release valve and a gauge to monitor the fuel pressure. The tank was also partitioned, and each compartment given its own fuel line. Although the SPAD XIII's radiator – like that of late-model SPAD VIIs – could be regulated by manually controlled shutters, early examples were prone to leakage until sturdier ones were quickly introduced, along with less rigid attachments that subjected them to reduced levels of stress.

Once the initial teething troubles had been ironed out, the SPAD XIII's firepower, combined with its ability to lose most pursuers in a dive – not only because of its speed, but because of the wing cellule's ability to hold up to the strain – made it popular with its pilots.

Although Britain had initially ordered 120 SPAD XIIIs, it only had 57 by April 1918, of which 16 were on strength with No. 23 Sqn. By then the newly organised Royal Air Force (RAF) had enough indigenously designed Hispano-Suiza-powered fighters, such as the SE 5a and the odd-looking, but excellent, Sopwith 5F1 Dolphin, to render the SPAD superfluous. On 4 May No. 23 Sqn replaced its SPADs with Dolphins. Thus, no British SPAD XIII ever met the Fokker D VII in combat, nor did any that the French shipped to Italy. France also sold 37 SPAD XIIIs to Belgium in March 1918, but little is known about their use by its 10e Escadrille.

One French ally that did use the SPAD XIII extensively in 1918 was the United States, which had failed to develop an effective fighter design of its own. The USAS initially purchased Nieuport 28s – rotary-engined fighters rejected by the French – until enough SPADs were available. Operated by the 1st Pursuit Group, the Nieuports gave their pilots the chance to acquire combat experience over the relatively quiet Toul sector from April to late June 1918. However, the unit suffered heavy casualties over Château Thierry in July when it went up against Fokker D VIIs flown by some of the best airmen in the Luftstreitskräfte.

The USAS got its first of an eventual 893 SPAD XIIIs in March 1918. Prior to that, several American volunteer pilots of the Lafayette Flying Corps (LFC) had already flown the twin-gun SPAD in combat, and the experience of men such as Charles J. Biddle, G. DeFreest Larner, William T. Ponder, David E. Putnam and Thomas G. Cassady, all of whom later transferred to the USAS, would prove invaluable to the newer pilots.

Following the collapse of the last German offensive on 18 July 1918, the 1st Pursuit Group began replacing its Nieuports with SPAD XIIIs. The group's 95th Aero Sqn drew first blood in the new fighter on 25 July, when 1Lt James Knowles Jr claimed a Fokker D VII near Bouvardes. The actual damage he inflicted on his opponent is dubious, but there is no disputing what squadronmate 1Lt Walter L. Avery achieved in the same dogfight when a lucky shot in the carburettor forced his antagonist to land in Allied lines. The captured German pilot turned out to be none other than

Ltn Karl Menckhoff, commander of Royal Saxon Jagdstaffel 72 and a holder of the *Orden Pour le Mérite* with 39 victories to his credit.

Back in the Toul sector, the 2nd Pursuit Group, led by Maj Davenport Johnson, was formed from the 13th, 22nd, 103rd and 139th Aero Sqns on 30 June. Both the 103rd, organised from the famed American volunteer escadrille SPA124 'Lafayette' on 18 February 1918, and the 139th had already seen combat in SPAD VIIs prior to supplementing and ultimately replacing them with XIIIs.

On 29 July the 103rd Aero Sqn's commander, Maj William Thaw, was given command of the 3rd Pursuit Group, comprising the 28th, 49th, 93rd and 213th Aero Sqns, at Vaucouleurs. Thaw, a founding father of the Escadrille Lafayette, appealed to Maj Johnson to allow his old unit to join the 3rd Pursuit, and this duly occurred on 6 August when the two groups exchanged the 49th for the 103rd. By September all three USAS pursuit groups were fully equipped with the SPAD XIII.

FOKKER D VII

Although 1917 had dawned brightly for German fighter pilots with the success of the Albatros D II and its successor the D III, the year ended with uncertainty and frustration. Following the debacle of 'Bloody April', the Allied fighter units had been acquiring a succession of superb aircraft – France's 180hp SPAD VII and 220hp SPAD XIII and Britain's Bristol F 2B Fighter, Royal Aircraft Factory SE 5a, Sopwith Triplane and Sopwith Camel. German efforts to counter them with successors to the Albatros D III had yielded one disappointment after another.

The Albatros D V was a more streamlined, lightened development of the D III. And like the latter, it suffered from the sesquiplane lower wing failings that had blighted the D III throughout its frontline career. Indeed, lower wing failure was even worse with the D V than it had been with the D III, the sesquiplane having the unnerving habit of twisting and breaking off during violent manoeuvring or when in a high-speed dive. An attempt to reinforce the airframe, in the form of the D Va, made the fighter heavier, thus reducing the aeroplane's performance, which was already little improved over the D III.

The Pfalz D III looked like a sesquiplane but was in fact a true biplane with a smaller two-spar lower wing. Although indisputably sturdier than the Albatros, the Pfalz, whose sleek fuselage was fashioned from diagonally wrapped plywood strips, was criticised for being heavy, underpowered and sluggish. Additionally, its machine guns, housed within the fuselage, were inaccessible to the pilot in the event of a jam. The later Pfalz D IIIa featured rounder, lower wingtips, an enlarged tailplane and guns more conventionally repositioned atop the fuselage, but the aeroplane never overcame its image among German fighter pilots as being little more than a secondary resort.

On its nose and partially stripped of fabric, a Fokker D VII displays details of its wooden cantilever wing structure, as well as the slightly off-centre angle of the vertical stabiliser which helped counter propeller torque. (Greg VanWyngarden)

SPAD XIII

20ft 6.5in.

8ft 6.333in.

26ft 7in.

Anthony Fokker's Dr I, ordered as a copy of the Sopwith Triplane but featuring an innovative wooden box wing structure that obviated the need for bracing wires, captured imaginations with its outstanding rate of climb and manoeuvrability. Early production models suffered structural failures due to poor quality control, however, and even after steps were taken to remedy that, the aeroplane was handicapped by German difficulties in supplying a suitable lubricant for its 110hp rotary engine. The Dr I was also slower than most of its Allied counterparts, except when climbing.

In spite of the shortcomings of their fighters, skill and superior tactics allowed the German pilots to hold their own throughout the year. They were aided by the essentially defensive war they were fighting, with prevailing westerly winds acting as a further handicap to Allied airmen striving to regain their side of the lines.

On 21 March 1918, however, it was the Germans who went over to the offensive with Operation *Michael* – the first phase of a last desperate bid for victory in the West. At that time the Luftsteitskräfte's best available fighter was the Fokker Dr I, fewer than 200 of which were available. Most were allocated to Jagdgeschwader I, II and III to serve as the 'tip of the spear', whose supporting shaft consisted of Albatros D Vs and D Vas and Pfalz D IIIs and D IIIas. By then rumours of better aircraft were reaching the beleaguered *Jagdflieger*, the first confirmations of which arrived in April in the form of the Siemens-Schuckert Werke (SSW) D III and the Fokker D VII.

In late January 1918, Idflieg had held a fighter competition at Berlin's Adlershof airfield. The 31 contestants from ten manufacturers ranged from improved versions of the Albatros D Va and Pfalz D IIIa, powered by the new high-compression straight-six Mercedes D IIIaü water-cooled engine, to original, innovative designs. One outstanding newcomer was SSW's D III, which used the 160hp Siemens und Halse Sh III 11-cylinder counter-rotary engine whose propeller and cylinders rotated in opposite directions to the crankshaft. This unusual configuration resulted in greater propeller and cooling efficiency, better fuel economy, reduced drag, lower weight and a greatly reduced gyroscopic effect.

Flown by Ltn Hans Müller on 21 January, the SSW D III displayed exhilarating manoeuverability and an impressive rate of climb. Idflieg ordered 30 D IIIs on 1 March, followed by 50 more on 23 March and 50 of the D IV – a variant with new wings of reduced span and equal chord (based on the D III's lower set) that sacrificed some of that climb rate for greater level speed – on 8 April.

JG II had 35 SSW D IIIs on strength by 18 May, and Jasta 19's commander, Lt d R Hans Pippart, probably used one to destroy a Breguet 14B.2 on the 20th. After seven to ten flying hours, however, mechanics began to report overheating, ejecting spark plugs, faulty magnetos, bearing failure, faulty throttles, disintegrating piston heads and complete engine seizures.

By 23 May JG II's SSWs had been withdrawn. D IIIs and D IVs began returning to frontline service on 22 July, their Sh IIIs having been replaced by Sh III(Rh) engines built under licence by the Rhenania Motorenfabrik AG (Rhemag), which curiously proved less troublesome than the originals. Even then, most of the 136 operational SSWs served in the interceptor role with home defence – *Kampfeinsitzer Staffeln*.

Anthony Fokker had sent no fewer than eight aircraft to Aldershof – the rotary-engined V9 biplane, the V11, V13 and V18 biplanes, the V17 and V20 monoplanes

OPPOSITE
SPAD XIII S7613 of 1Lt Leslie J Rummell, 93rd Aero Sqn, based at Vaucouleurs, October 1918. Rummell flew his third assigned SPAD from 23 September 1918 to the end of the war, being credited with two Fokker D VIIs and an Albatros two-seater on 29 September, and more D VIIs on 10, 23 and 29 October. It also outlasted him— Rummell died of influenza on 2 February 1919, while S7613 was condemned at the 1st Air Depot on 24 March.

OPPOSITE
Fokker D VII (F) 4264/18 of
Ltn d R Aloys Heldmann, Jasta
10 based at Marville, October
1918. The replacement for his
Mercedes-powered Fokker D VII
244/18, BMW-engined D VII (F)
4264/18 is reconstructed here
from Heldmann's description,
combining the usual Jasta 10
cowling with a blue fuselage
and blue and white
checquered tailplane.
Heldmann scored 10 of his 15
victories—including six SPAD
XIIIs—in D VIIs and died on 1
November 1983, aged 87.

When the first Fokker D VIIs
arrived at Jasta 10, Ltn Fritz
Friedrichs overshot in 234/18,
hit the D VII to the right of the
photograph (note that it is
missing much of its lower
right wing) and came to
rest amongst some tents.
(Greg VanWyngarden)

and two Dr I triplanes. Notwithstanding the attention that the SSW D III attracted, it was Fokker's V11 and V18 that won the competition.

Based on the Dr I, the V11 featured a biplane version of its wooden box spar wing and a 180hp Mercedes D IIIaü engine. The lower wing was smaller than the upper to improve downward visibility, and it was built in one piece, with a cutout arranged in the steel tube fuselage frame to accommodate it. The ailerons, installed on the upper wing only, were fabric-covered steel tube. The interplane and cabane struts were streamlined steel tubing. The V11 also featured a car-type radiator mounted in the nose, rather than on the fuselage sides or the upper wing.

Although impressed by the V11's performance during early test flights, JG I's commander, Rittm Manfred von Richthofen, reported it to be directionally unstable and prone to fall into a spin. Fokker responded by lengthening the fuselage by 40cm and adding a vertical stabiliser to produce the V18. Both aircraft were tested at the January 1918 competition, where von Richthofen and numerous other German fighter pilots unanimously praised the biplane's overall performance, including its ability to retain its manoeuvrability at high altitude and to 'hang on its prop'.

The V21 was a final refinement on the V18, the aircraft boasting a smaller triangular vertical stabiliser. It was this version that was accepted for production under the military designation of D VII, Fokker receiving a contract to build 400 fighters at a cost of 25,000 marks apiece. Much to his personal satisfaction after having been eclipsed by Albatros since September 1916, Anthony Fokker saw the Johannisthal (Albatros) and Schneidemühl (Ostdeutsche Albatros Werke, or OAW) factories of his bitter rivals ordered to manufacture the D VII under licence, with a five percent royalty going to Fokker.

D VIIs began arriving at Jasta 10 of JG I in late April 1918. Eagerly anticipating its arrival, von Richthofen had only allocated Dr Is to Jastas 6 and 11 when Operation *Michael* commenced, while Jastas 4 and 10 retained their inline-engined Albatros and Pfalz fighters to ensure a smooth pilot transition to the D VII. Although the 'Red Baron' avidly looked forward to flying the D VII in combat himself, he never got the chance to prior to being killed in action on 21 April.

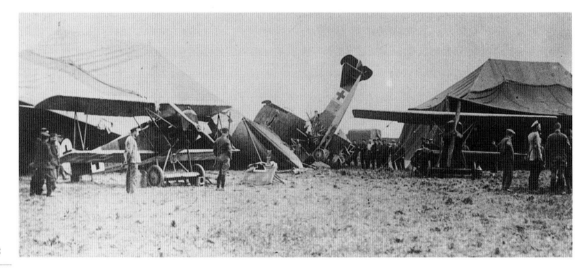

FOKKER D VII (F)

22ft 11.5in.

9ft 2.25in.

29ft 3.5in.

Ltn de R Aloys Heldmann of Jasta 10 claimed to have flown a D VII in combat in mid-April, and he brought down an SE 5a of No. 24 Sqn on 4 May (2Lt R. A. Slipper was taken prisoner), but it is most likely that he was still flying a Pfalz D IIIa at the time. His *Staffelführer*, Ltn Erich Löwenhardt, is known to have flown a D VII on the 9th, as implied by Ltn Richard Wenzl, then a Dr I pilot of Jasta 11, when he described an engagement between JG I fighters and British aircraft that afternoon in his 1930 memoir, *Richthofen Flieger*. 'To my left, Löwenhardt in his new biplane already had one in front of him.'

Löwenhardt claimed an SE 5a over Hamel at 1950 hrs for his 19th victory. This may have again been from No. 24 Sqn, whose 'C' Flight fought a 15–20 minute engagement over Bois de Hangard, although it lost no aeroplanes. RAF pilots from the unit in turn claimed three Albatros D Vs, and they did not report encountering any new types during the course of the combat. Löwenhardt had a less disputable success at 2030 hrs the next evening when he downed a DH 9 over Chaulnes, killing Lts L. E. Dunnett and H. D. Prosser of No. 27 Sqn.

On 18 May, Wenzl, who had transferred from Jasta 11 to Jasta 6 24 hours earlier, flew to 2. Armee Flug Park to exchange his Fokker Dr I for a D VII. Besides the superior speed and high-altitude performance that the new fighter offered, Wenzl recalled everyone being pleased to be returning to stationary, water-cooled engines. 'The inferior Rizinus oil – the elixir of life for rotary engines – made it so apparent that on hot days there would be no end to the forced landings.'

Jasta 10 aces Ltns Fritz Friedrichs (left) and Erich Löwenhardt pose before a captured SPAD XIII of SPA88 in June 1918. Löwenhardt may have scored the first D VII victories on 9 and 10 May 1918, but Friedrichs was killed baling out of one on 15 July. (Greg VanWyngarden)

By the end of May 1918, D VIIs had become the mainstays at Jastas 6, 10 and 11, while Jasta 4 operated castoff triplanes from Jastas 6 and 11 until more of the new Fokker fighters reached the front.

While JG I's pilots familiarised themselves with their D VIIs, and downed two SPAD VIIs on 19 May, their commander, Hptm Wilhelm Reinhard, received orders on the 21st to depart Cappy aerodrome for Pusieux Ferme, from whence they would support the 7. Armee's offensive on the Chemin des Dames. JG I arrived at Pusieux on the evening of the 26th, but poor weather limited operations when the German spring offensive's third phase, Operation *Blücher-Yorck*, commenced on 27 May.

Amid the day's confusion a mystery arose. The British reportedly found Fokker D VII serial No. 2184/18 near Achiet-le-Grand, and gave it the captured aircraft registration number G/5/12. The only German loss that matches the acquisition is that of Ltn d R Rudolf Windisch, commander of Jasta 66, who was brought down while attacking a French aerodrome, probably by Sous-Lt Souleau and M d L Cavieux of SPA76.

Vzfw Erich Sonneck of Jasta 66 poses before Ltn Rudolf Windisch's new Fokker (OAW) D VII 2035/18, bearing a white stag over a yellow shield and what is undoubtedly a band in Saxon green and white. (Greg VanWyngarden)

Windisch, who was credited with a SPAD before going down, had been photographed shortly prior to his demise in the cockpit of a D VII marked with a leaping stag on the fuselage side, suggesting that as a seasoned *Kanone*, he had the rare privilege (for an *Amerika-Programm* unit member at that time) of receiving one of the new fighters. Maybe it was his aeroplane, or the remains thereof, that were recovered by the British in the sector?

Adding to the day's anomalies were conflicting reports that Windisch was a prisoner, and that he had subsequently been killed – shot while trying to escape, perhaps? In any case, the Fokker D VII did not remain secret for long.

Meanwhile, at JG II's base at Le Mesnil-Nesle, Hptm Rudolf Berthold had also been looking forward to his *Staffeln* getting D VIIs, but even the delivery of his own machine was delayed. On 28 May JG I lent him one of its Fokker fighters, and he took to it instantly. 'It flies very comfortably', he noted. 'Above all, the controls are so light that I can even handle them with my right arm.' Given the fact that a neglected, still-festering wound rendered his right arm all but useless, Berthold's comments speak volumes for the D VII's handling characteristics – as does the fact that he used it to shoot down a Breguet 14 over Crouy later that same morning.

The next afternoon Berthold was again leading Jasta 15's Albatros D Vas in his 'borrowed' machine when they were jumped north of Ville-en-Tardenois by SPADs of SPA77. The French unit's star turn, Sous-Lt Maurice Boyau, who had burned a German kite balloon over Bois de Dole earlier that day, now shared in the credit for an Albatros downed and a second that went unconfirmed. Evidently, SPA77's Jasta 15 victims survived, but the same cannot be said for Sgt André Gelin, whose SPAD XIII became the first of its type to fall victim to a Fokker D VII when Berthold turned the tables on his ambushers and shot Gelin down south of Soissons at 1620 hrs. Ten minutes later Ltn Josef Veltjens was credited with a second SPAD and Ltn Georg von Hantelmann with a 'probable', but in reality Gelin was SPA77's only loss. At 1640 hrs Berthold topped the day off by claiming a Salmson 2A2, probably from SAL27.

The next few days saw another initial surge in German fortunes on the ground, as Château-Thierry fell to the 7. Armee on 30 May and JG I moved up to occupy the former French aerodrome at Beugneux-Cremaille on 1 June. In the air, the last few days of May saw the Fokker D VII burst into almost instant prominence. Known successes for the fighter on the 31st included Breguets by Jasta 6's Ltn d R Hans Kirschstein and Ltn Martin Skowronski and a SPAD credited to the *Geschwaderführer*, Hptm Reinhard. June saw a proliferation of Fokker D VIIs over the front, accompanied by glowing reports from their pilots and awed reactions from their Allied opponents.

Ltn d Rudolf Windisch did not fly D VII 2035/18 long before being downed by the French – and his fighter ultimately turned up in British records. (Greg VanWyngarden)

Jagdgeschwader II commander Oblt Rudolf Berthold (centre, facing the camera), seen here in 1917 amid his pilots of Jasta 18, used a Fokker D VII borrowed from JG I to score the type's first success over a SPAD XIII. (Jon Guttman)

TECHNICAL
SPECIFICATIONS

SPAD XIII

The SPAD XIII displayed impressive speed and climb – whenever the reduction gear of its Hispano-Suiza 8B engine was not failing. The rounded wingtips on the early XIIIs produced by SPAD and Blériot displayed inferior lateral control compared to the SPAD VII, however, so they were soon redesigned to the latter's original, angular configuration for subsequent production batches. In an attempt to provide a similar improvement in handling to existing fighters while newer ones made their way to the front, SPAD issued triangular three-ply 'pockets' that could be sewed onto the ailerons and fore and aft wingtips – 300+ XIIIs were so modified in the winter of 1918.

This early Blériot-built SPAD XIII of SPA155, probably flown by unit commander Capt Edmond George, displays the 'pocket' extensions sewn onto the wing and aileron tips to square off their contours. (SHAA)

All but one of the SPAD XIIIs issued to No. 23 Sqn in December 1917 had rounded wingtips, which the French also offered to retro-fit with the wooden 'pockets'. The British declined, however, because after evaluating the 'quick fix' the RFC representative in the Paris officer of the Ministry of Munitions stated, 'The execution of the work is badly carried out, and should the twine rot or fray, the three-ply corner would become detached, probably jamming or damaging the aileron'.

In spite of this jaundiced British appraisal, early model SPAD XIIIs with pocket extensions on their wings continued to turn up in French and American squadrons well into 1918. An artifact providing proof is SPAD XIII S7689 *Smith IV* of the 22nd Aero Sqn in which 1Lt Arthur Raymond Brooks scored his sixth victory on October 1918. This aircraft, which is now preserved at the National Air and Space Museum in Washington, DC, has an upper wing of the later, squared-off shape, but a replacement lower wing of the early, rounded configuration with pocket extensions.

Seeking an alternative to the Hispano-Suiza 8B, SPAD experimented with installing a 200hp Renault 8Gd in a SPAD XIII airframe, but nothing came of it.

Capt René Fonck poses before a SPAD XVII, which displays an enlarged radiator and cowling to accommodate its 300hp Hispano-Suiza 8Fb engine and extra bracing wires extending to the undercarriage. Only 20 were built, and they saw limited use by GC 12 in the war's last weeks. (SHAA B81.1397)

SPAD XIII	Early model	Late model	
Dimensions			
Length	20ft 6.5in	20ft 6.5in	
Height	8ft 6.333in	8ft 6.333in	
Span	27ft 8in	26ft 7in	
Wing Area	227.226 sq. ft	217.430 sq. ft	
Weight			
Empty	1,326lb	–	
Loaded	1,888lb	–	
Performance	**SPAD XIII**	**SPAD XIII**	**SPAD XVII**
Engine	220hp	220hp	300hp
	Hispano-Suiza	Hispano-Suiza	Hispano-Suiza
	8Ba, 8Bb or 8Bd	8BBc or 8Be	8Fb
Maximum speed (mph)			
3,280ft	131.2	–	–
6,560ft	129.6	135.5	134.8
9,840ft	127.7	–	133
13,120ft	124.9	–	131.2
16,400ft	118.1	–	124.9

Climb to	min	sec	min	sec	min	sec
3,280ft	2	20	–	–	–	–
6,560ft	5	17	4	40	5	24
9,840ft	8	45	–	–	8	20
13,120ft	13	5	–	–	12	32
16,400ft	20	10	–	–	17	21
Service ceiling	22,360ft		–		–	
Endurance (hours)	1¾		–		–	

At least one SPAD (S706) was fitted with a Rateau supercharger, located behind the pilot's seat, but in spite of an alleged top speed of 139.8mph, its overall performance was reportedly inferior to the standard aeroplane's.

In early 1918, the Aviation Militaire requested a fighter with a more powerful engine than the Spad XIII's. Hispano-Suiza responded with the 300hp 8Fb, and SPAD created a stronger airframe to accept it. The result was the SPAD 17.C1, whose dimensions were virtually identical to the XIII's, but which featured a larger engine cowling and more stringers to round out the fuselage behind it. The wing cellule was reinforced to a factor of nine, with added bracing wires running under the lower wing to the undercarriage. The fighter's horizontal stabilisers were also enlarged.

Most of the test batch of 20 SPAD XVIIs served with Groupe de Combat 12 in late 1918, but their performance proved to be only marginally better than the XIII's, so in 1919 the Aviation Militaire adopted the Nieuport 29 as its standard fighter instead.

THE 'FLYING BRICK'

The first SPAD XIIIs to arrive at the 95th Aero Sqn on 25 July 1918 were welcomed by pilots who hoped that their greater power and robust structure would offer an advantage over the Nieuport 28, with its volatile Gnome monosoupape rotary engine and wing fabric that was prone to tearing away in a dive. Pilots from the 94th shared those sentiments as well, but the aviators manning the 27th and 147th Aero Sqns, led by RFC veterans who were more accustomed to the Nieuports' limitations, and how to adapt to them, were less enthusiastic.

Maj Harold E. Hartney, Canadian-born commander of the 27th Aero Sqn, wrote, 'An Englishman who flew one of the SPADs on our aerodrome said, "The thing flies like a 'bloody brick', you know"'. That was our opinion, too, and it remained with us through to the end of the war'. The 'flying brick' sobriquet referred to the fact that the SPAD's greater weight and thinner wing cross section gave it a higher wing loading than that of the light, docile Nieuport 28. This in turn meant that the fighter had a steeper glide angle, which normally required the engine to be running at high speed in order for the pilot to land the SPAD XIII safely. Charles R. D'Olive of the 93rd Aero Sqn agreed:

> The SPADs were wonderful aeroplanes after you learned how to fly them. For the novice, they had the gliding angle and the stability of a brick. After you learned how to fly them you could hang them on a tight turn pretty nice. You had to fly them with the engine.

While the Americans complained about the SPAD's 'hot' landing characteristics, Swiss volunteer, and five-victory ace, Jacques R. Roques of SPA48 claimed to have developed a technique that saw him glide his SPAD in by raising the nose during final

Upper cowling details of 1Lt A Raymond Brooks' SPAD XIII as it undergoes restoration at the Smithsonian Institution. (Greg VanWyngarden)

SPAD XIII COCKPIT

1. Faired-over water and auxiliary fuel pipes
2. Crétien gunsight
3. 0.303-in Vickers machine guns
4. Charging handles
5. Radiator cap
6. Clearance recess for charging handles
7. Windscreen
8. Ammunition discharge chute
9. Magneto switch
10. Air pump emergency shut-off

11. Fuel tank selector
12. Air pump selector/air pressure release
13. Speedometer
14. Altimeter
15. Air pressure gauge
16. Tachometer
17. Water temperature
18. Oil pressure
19. Air pressure regulator
20. Throttle and fuel regulator

21. Compass
22. Rudder bar
23. Control column with triggers
24. Mallet
25. Fuel gauge
26. Fuel tank cap
27. Seat
28. Starting magneto
29. Oil tank cap

approach to slow it down, prior to levelling off just before touchdown and effecting a smooth landing. In regard to the matter of landing, however, seven-victory ace French ace Jean Fraissinet flatly stated 'I don't have any memory of the excessive landing speeds you bring up'.

The other principal complaint against the SPAD XIII, from French and American pilots alike, concerned the unreliability of the Hispano-Suiza 8B engine, with its failure-prone spur reduction gear. 'Even our mechanics, the very best in the world, could not keep them as serviceable as the Nieuports', Maj Hartney stated. 'Therefore, our "machines available" for each day's work dropped from about 90 per cent to 50 per cent, despite long hours of night work and extra men on each job.'

While Hispano-Suiza strove to refine the quality of the 8B engine, the principal means of making the SPAD XIII an effective fighter was constant maintenance by the groundcrews. Hartney, as CO of the 27th Aero Sqn and later the 1st Pursuit Group, gave due recognition to the critical role played by those oft-overlooked men:

> Although it meant four days for a complete overhaul of the new water-cooled engine against four hours on the air-cooled Monosoupape, they realised the additional risks being taken by the pilots and accepted the situation with good grace.

If its pilots thought the SPAD XIII flew like a brick, it dived like a brick, too. And when it needed to, the ability of its solid wing structure to hold together came to be appreciated by any hard-pressed SPAD pilot who found himself outclimbed or outmanoeuvred by one or more Fokker D VIIs.

'I never knew one to fall apart', said Charles D'Olive. 'I know a fellow who got credit for two Fokkers that followed him in a dive. When he pulled out they tried to pull out after him and they left their wings there. He didn't fire a shot, but he got credit for two Fokkers.'

The tactics devised to make the most of the SPAD XIII's strengths and minimise its weaknesses – similar to those employed by American pilots to outfight more nimble Japanese aircraft during World War II – were described in a letter home by Sgt Charles J. Biddle, dated 23 November 1917. An LFC member of N73, he subsequently had the privilege of using a new SPAD XIII to score his first victory over a two-seater on 5 December:

> You may think it sounds foolish, or as if one was blowing a bit of talk about attacking five when we were only two, but an attack does not necessarily mean that you charge into the middle of them and mix it up. On the contrary you can, by diving at high speed from above, get in some shots and then by using your great speed climb up above them again out of reach before they get in a shot. If you remember to leave your motor on as you are diving, and in this way to come down as fast as possible, without at the same time going so fast as to interfere with your shooting, the great speed gained in this way will enable you to make a short, steep climb. You can thus regain a position perhaps 200 metres above the heads of the Huns, where they cannot effectively shoot at you. I am now of course speaking only of an attack on a group of single-seater machines.

A French SPAD XIII with a bullet hole through its windscreen shows a wealth of upper cowling detail. (Blaine Pardoe)

If the engagement ends here, the chances of bringing one down are not great, but you can sometimes by such methods and by, for instance, hitting some part of one of the machines, so worry the Huns that one will get separated from his comrades in the general confusion so that you can get a fair crack at him.

The advantage in level and especially diving speed that the SPAD XIII held over even the BMW-engined Fokker D VII was attested to by Ltn Richard Wenzl of Jasta 6 as he described several combats he had with American fighters on 30 October 1918:

The scene was always the same. A tight turn and then the SPAD pilots were overtaken, but they saved themselves by going into a vertical nosedive. Naturally, we couldn't follow them, so we forced an entire SPAD flight of seven aircraft down in turn. My rage over this bunch knew no bounds.

Ltn Friedrich Noltenius, serving with Jasta 6 on 9 October, also noted that during an encounter with SPADs that day, 'I attacked them one after the other but without hitting them. One of them was able to catch me off guard, but he shot miserably. I learned that I was unable to gain on the 200hp SPAD, even with the BMW engine.'

Later, improved production batches of SPAD XIIIs left fonder memories among those who flew them. 'The SPAD was an awfully comfortable aeroplane to fly', recalled Leighton Brewer of the 13th Aero Sqn, 'as it had a large cockpit, and the heat from the water-cooled engine kept the pilot warm up to 5,000 metres. It was a wonderful aeroplane to fight in – probably the best fighter aeroplane developed during World War I.'

Brewer's SPAD, which bore the personal number '3', served throughout his time at the front with five different engines, of which he stated:

The first two were very good and the last three not so good. The first one lasted 60 hours and the second 40 hours when I cracked a cylinder over the lines and had to go back home. I had my aeroplane fixed up to suit me. I have pretty small hands, and had a hard time squeezing both machine gun triggers at the same time. I had my mechanic turn one around to put them closer together. I had the instruments placed just where I wanted them, and also had a piece of iron put under the seat.

FOKKER D VII

After receiving a Fokker D VII with a 180hp Mercedes IIIaü engine on 18 May, Ltn Richard Wenzl of Jasta 11 gave it an initial appraisal:

> We were astounded at what Fokker had been able to wring out of the long-outdated Mercedes engine. The new biplane was not as manoeuvrable as our triplanes, but it was somewhat speedier. It was a little slow climbing at low altitude, but it climbed better at high altitude, as we had installed the high-compression engines that were designed for high altitude.

As Wenzl noted, JG I's pilots were pleased to return to oil-lubricated stationary engines after the unreliability displayed by the castor oil-lubricated rotaries of their Fokker Dr Is. Ltn Fritz Friedrichs of Jasta 10 also learned of the D VII's inherent structural soundness when an exploding anti-aircraft shell broke a lower wing spar in half, but the overall wing cellule held until he flew home. About that time Wenzl was also fired upon by one of his own *Staffel* mates whilst dogfighting with SE 5as, but he called it 'a forgivable mistake because the D VII did bear a certain similarity to the SE 5'.

Many of the D VII's virtues lay in its cantilever wing, whose thicker airfoil and high aspect ratio gave it a lift coefficient of 1.1, compared to 1.0 for the SPAD, and consequently a superior rate of climb. Its horn-balanced control surfaces also reduced control forces, endowing it with a rare combination of outstanding agility and forgiving ease.

There seemed to be only three things wrong with the D VII. Elated though they were with their first D VIIs using the 180hp Mercedes IIIaü, many pilots thought it would benefit from a better engine – and later that summer it got two. Mercedes

As with most German fighter pilots of 1918, Ltn Richard Wenzl, *Staffelführer* of Jasta 6, was elated to receive both the Mercedes- and later BMW-engined Fokker D VIIs. He scored most of his 12 victories in the aircraft. (Greg VanWyngarden)

The Mercedes D III engine was installed in most German fighters from 1916 through to 1918, including the Fokker D VII. Powered by the higher-compression IIIaü, the D VII was a very good fighter, but the BMW IIIa made it a great one. (Greg VanWyngarden)

produced the 200hp IIIaüv, but it was the Fokker D VII (F), powered by the 185hp BMW IIIa, that exhibited the most stellar performance, especially at altitudes of 18,000ft or above. This combination truly made it the terror of the Western Front, as Ltn Wenzl recalled:

> On 22 June the first BMW Fokkers arrived and were issued to Jasta 11. The aces each got one as well. I led the *Staffel* while Kirschstein was in Berlin, and I tried out his BMW, which pleased me greatly. This machine easily reached 6,000 metres in 24 minutes – that was a tremendous feat in those days. The effects of these new machines immediately became evident. Staffel 11 was once more shooting down a good many machines because it was now an easy thing to overtake and shoot down those French reconnaissance aeroplanes that flew extraordinarily high.

A second more disturbing flaw was a tendency for the D VII's ammunition to overheat and explode within the confines of its front cowling. On 15 July 1918, Fokker D VII 309/18, flown by Ltn Fritz Friedrichs (Jasta 10's balloon specialist with eleven aeroplanes and ten 'gasbags' to his credit, suddenly burst into flame, most likely due to the spontaneous combustion of his phosphorus rounds. When his fuel tank exploded Friedrichs abandoned his aeroplane, but his parachute caught on the tailplane and ripped, causing him to plunge to his death.

Fellow JG I pilot Ltn d R Julius Bender of Jasta 4 had a similar experience the next day when his ammunition went off, setting his D VII (2063/18) afire. Bender took to his parachute at an altitude of just 200 metres and was fortunate to alight with only a sprained ankle. Improved ammunition was the ultimate remedy to the problem, but a common interim precaution was to cut ventilating holes or louvres in the cowling in a manner that varied from one Jasta to another.

The Fokker D VII's third and arguably most vocally expressed fault was that there never seemed to be enough of them to satisfy demand, and the fighters produced to supplement them almost invariably suffered in comparison when appraised by the pilots who had to settle for them.

In mid-May early examples of the LFG Roland D VI, featuring a fuselage built up of wooden clinkers like a boat, were assigned to Jastas 23b, 32b, 33 and 35b. Its performance was no better than that of the Albatros D Va, and in late May Jasta 23b's commander, Lt d R Otto Kissenberth, flew a captured Sopwith Camel in preference to his unit's LFG Rolands! The SSW D III and D IV were well accepted once their engine problems were rectified, but their most striking virtue, their rate of climb, as

Behind the whimsical face on Oblt Hermann Pritsch's D VII of Jasta 17 are ventilating holes added to the cowling to reduce the disconcerting possibility of spontaneous ignition of his ammunition. The positions and shapes of such apertures varied from aeroplane to aeroplane and *Staffel* to *Staffel*.
(Greg VanWyngarden)

well as continued German doubts about the reliability of rotary engines in general, resulted in them being allocated more often to home defence *Kampfeinsitzer Staffeln* than to frontline *Jastas*.

August saw the appearance of the Pfalz D XII at the front. Although its frontal radiator frequently led Allied pilots to mistake it for the Fokker D VII, the new Pfalz featured the same semi-monocoque plywood fuselage as the earlier D III, while its wings, of a drag-reducing thin aerofoil section inspired by the SPAD, were conventionally wire-braced with two bays of N-shaped interplane struts.

In his postwar memoir *Jagdstaffel Unsere Heimat*, Ltn Rudolf Stark mentioned that his command, Jasta 35b, accepted Pfalz D XIIs on 1 September 'only after much discussion and long telephone conversations', and that every pilot 'climbed into the new machine with preconceived notions and immediately voiced all manner of complaints'. His mechanics were already so 'spoiled' by the Fokker D VII's cantilever wings that they complained of the renewed labour required to keep the Pfalz's guy wires adjusted between missions. Later, Stark admitted, the Pfalz D XII turned out to be a fairly good aeroplane that 'climbed well and could fly along with the Fokker D VII in all respects, and in a dive it was a bit faster. But in turns and combat it was slow and could not compare with the Fokkers.'

Statistics aside, the Fokker D VII had set a new standard in the Luftstreitskräfte. By the end of June 1918 virtually every other fighter of its generation was comparatively judged against that standard, and most were found wanting.

Dimensions				
Span	29ft 3.5in			
Length	22ft 11.5in			
Height	9ft 2.25in			
Wing Area	221.4 sq. ft			
Weights				
Empty	1,474lb			
Loaded	2,112lb			
Performance				
Powerplant	Mercedes IIIaü (180hp)		BMW IIIa (185hp)	
Maximum speed (mph)	118.1		125	
Climb to	min	sec	min	sec
3,280ft	4	15	1	40
6,560ft	8	18	7	5
9,840ft	13	49	7	0
13,120ft	22	48	10	15
16,400ft	38	5	15	30
Service Ceiling	20,000ft		24,280ft	
Endurance (hours)	1½		–	

FOKKER VERSUS SPAD

On 3 July 1918, the American 1st Pursuit Group received the following intelligence report from the French VI Armée, under whose auspices it was then serving in the Château Thierry sector:

> The triplane Fokker is disappearing little by little. The Fokker D VII (biplane) is reported by our pursuit pilots to be encountered frequently. It is an excellent machine, being better than the 180hp SPAD and equal to the 220hp SPAD in horizontal speed, and it is apparently able to climb faster, is extremely manoeuvrable and able to continue acrobacy at high altitudes of 5000 to 5500 metres.

By then the Americans had already learned what the 'square nose', as they also called the D VII, could do against their Nieuport 28s, with the added misfortune of having had to face some of the best pilots the Germans could put in them. The arrival of SPAD XIIIs in July was greeted with mixed feelings in the 1st Pursuit Group, and the SPADs' first clashes with Fokkers were equally mixed, combining encouraging successes with the frustration of all too frequent engine failures.

Even when victorious, American pilots regarded the D VII as an adversary to respect. On 10 October 1Lt Richard D. Shelby of the 139th Aero Sqn had dropped out of his patrol with a rough-running engine and was circling over the lines to await his comrades' return when he noticed five or six aeroplanes making diving passes at the trenches below. Diving to take position behind them, he identified them as 'Fokkers from the Checkerboard Circus', painted in red and white squares. Those

Fokker D VII (F) 7788/18, delivered to Coblenz on 2 January 1919 for testing by the USAS, displays its 185hp BMW IIIa engine, as well as the five-colour lozenge camouflage pattern printed on the fabric. (R. Watts Album via Greg VanWyngarden)

FOKKER D VII COCKPIT

1. 7.62mm LMG 08/15 machine guns
2. Fuel gauge
3. Ring and bead sights
4. Fuel tank cap
5. Ammunition chutes
6. Ammunition feeds
7. Gun padding
8. Tachometer
9. Magneto switch
10. Main fuel tank pressure gauge
11. Auxiliary fuel tank pressure gauge
12. Oil pump switch
13. Magneto switch
14. Fuel tank switch
15. Main fuel pump switch
16. Auxiliary tank fuel pump switch
17. Throttle control handle
18. Ignition control handle
19. Rudder control bar
20. Auxiliary throttle
21. Machine gun buttons
22. Control column grip
23. Hand fuel pump
24. Control column
25. Compass
26. Leather-covered aluminium seat

D VIIs were the best fighter aeroplanes produced during the war, certainly at low altitude', he said, 'and these were flown by veterans. By the time I realised who they were, things were happening so fast I didn't have time to be scared'. Closing on the rearmost Fokker, Shelby fired at close range and followed it down as the fighter dived, streaming white vapour, until his guns jammed:

> Although he crashed inside our lines, I didn't actually see it because I was so busy trying to apply immediate action to my guns. The first indication that I was in trouble came when my instrument panel exploded in my face. I didn't know where the shot had come from, so I twisted around to look over my shoulder, and my heart caught in my throat. There, a dozen yards behind me and square on my tail, was one of the Fokkers with the muzzles of both guns flickering. When you are in trouble in a SPAD, you dive, so I dived.

In spite of shot-up controls, Shelby managed to pull out of his 200mph dive just above the Meuse River, his propeller kicking up spray as he did so. Barely clearing the riverbank, he flew past Verdun and spotted a small field. 'I fishtailed straight in and made a pretty good landing', he conluded. 'The aeroplane was shot up but otherwise in pretty good shape.'

No German loss corresponds to Shelby's third accredited victory, for which he received the Distinguished Service Cross (DSC), but he may in turn have been the tenth victory claimed by Oblt Theodor Cammann of Jasta 74, whose aeroplanes are known to have sported chequered markings.

A superb view of the cockpit of D VII 4635/18 undergoing restoration at the Smithsonian Institution. The fuel gauge lies between the gun barrels, while the rev counter is between the breeches. To the left of the lefthand gun is the grease pump for the engine water pump. The brown handle forward of the fuel gauge is the decompression lever to ease starting the engine. (Greg VanWyngarden)

THE STRATEGIC
SITUATION

The SPAD XIII's arrival on the Western Front in the late summer of 1917 attended the series of Allied offensives that bogged down by the end of the year. In the months that followed, as the French strove to deliver the new fighter in quantity even while correcting its flaws, the Germans were also mobilising and upgrading their ground and air assets for a grand strike of their own.

With revolution-wracked Russia out of the war and the Italians reeling back to the Piave River in the wake of their disastrous defeat at Caporetto on 26 October 1917, the Germans saw what could be a final opportunity to force France and Britain to sue for peace before their American allies reached the front in force. By the time the Fokker D VII entered operational service in the late spring of 1918, that critical effort was already in progress.

The American declaration of war against Germany on 6 April 1917 had already affected the Luftstreitskräfte, compelling it to initiate what it dubbed the *Amerika-Programm* in June. On paper, this doubled the number of *Jagdstaffeln* in anticipation of whatever the US Army fielded in the course of the year, and it was to be lent substance through the accelerated development of a new generation of state-of-the-art fighters. The training programme was also drastically expanded by the addition of a second fighter school, Jastaschule II, alongside Jastaschule I at Valenciennes/Fâmars on 8 August 1917, followed by the newer school's relocation to Nivelles in February 1918.

By the time Operation *Michael* was launched on 21 March 1918, however, the Luftstreitskräfte's best fighter was still the Fokker Dr I, serving primarily with the three crack *Jagdgeschwader* while the other *Jagdstaffeln* got by on Albatros D Vs and

D Vas and Pfalz D IIIs and D IIIas. The discrepancy in fighting quality was especially marked in the hastily created *Amerika-Programm Jagdstaffeln*, which usually consisted of a veteran commander and perhaps a small cadre of experienced men, surrounded by hastily trained pilots who would duly have to complete their apprenticeship in battle against the Allies.

On top of their usually being understrength, the newer *Jastas* also had older, sometimes obsolescent, hand-me-down fighters in which their neophyte pilots would have to acquire whatever combat experience they could the hard way – rendered all the harder by the generally superior quality, as well as quantity, of their opponents' machines by this stage of the war.

Although the more experienced German aviators flew their aeroplanes with great tactical skill and élan, their British counterparts fought back with confidence in the intrinsic superiority of their own fighters, namely the Sopwith Camel and Dolphin, the SE 5a and the Bristol F 2B. Likewise, the French retained confidence in their reliable, still-capable SPAD VIIs, even if the progressively more numerous SPAD XIII, with its troublesome Hispano-Suiza 8B engine, was continuing to attract mixed reviews. In November 1917, for example, a number of *escadrilles* had reported that their SPAD XIIIs were grounded for two days out of three because of persistent engine trouble.

The first USAS fighter units to see action – the 94th and 95th Aero Sqns – had commenced operations in the relatively quiet Toul sector on 31 March 1918. They were equipped with Nieuport 28s until a sufficient number of SPAD XIIIs became available to replace them. The 103rd Aero Sqn, created directly from the all-volunteer Escadrille SPA124 'Lafayette' on 18 February 1918, used a mixed bag of SPAD VIIs and XIIIs over the Champagne and Flanders fronts, as did the 139th Aero Sqn in the Toul sector in July.

The final German offensive along the Marne on 15 July 1918 pitted all three *Jagdgeschwader* and other crack Fokker D VII-equipped *Jastas* against the most seasoned *Groupes de Combat* and *escadrilles* of French Escadre I, as well as the American 1st Pursuit Group, operating from Saints with Nieuport 28s until the 95th Aero Sqn committed its new SPAD XIIIs to the fight on 25 July.

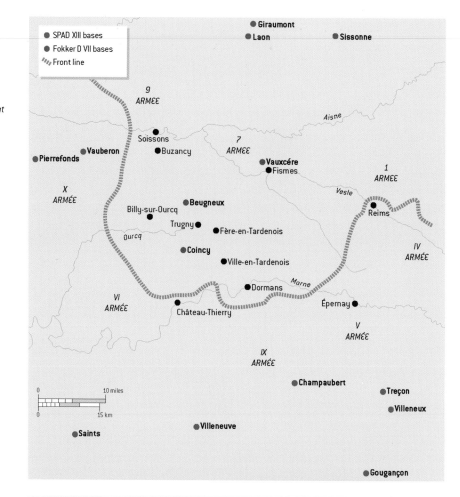

Members of Groupe de Combat 18 at Montdidier rest between strafing missions before some SPAD XIIIs of SPA48. From left are: Lt Jean Gigodot, CO, SPA153 (4 victories), Sgt Michel Bellaigue, SPA153, Lt Roger Cael, SPA48, Adh Auguste Binoche, SPA48 (3), SLt André Barcat, SPA153 (5), Adj Raymond Boudou, SPA48 (2), MdL Georges Halberger, SPA153 (5), SLt Marie Gilbert de Guingand, SPA48 (8), Sgt Rémy Morel, SPA153, Col Alexandre Mercier, SPA48 (2), SLt Robert Bajac, SPA48 (4) and Adj Jean Marie Danglade, SPA48 (1) (SHAA B93.1078)

When the Fokker D VII finally made its combat debut in May 1918, the German offensive was about to enter its third phase, with the element of surprise and much of the initiative already lost. In spite of some early German successes, the Allies showed no sign of collapsing, and at the end of June the USAS committed its 1st Pursuit Group, consisting of the 27th, 94th, 95th and 147th Aero Sqns, to the Château Thierry sector.

The Americans had gained considerable experience, and confidence in Toul during the spring of 1918, but their opposition there had been second-rate Albatros and Pfalz-equipped *Amerika-Programm Jagdstaffeln*. Throughout July the Fokker D VIIs, flown by some of Germany's best surviving pilots, ran roughshod over the hapless Nieuport 28s. SPAD XIIIs finally began to reach the 1st Pursuit Group in mid-July, and the 95th subsequently claimed the group's first successes with the new fighter type on the 25th.

By then the last German bid for victory had been irretrievably lost, a final push over the Marne having been repulsed on 18 July. From then on it was the Allies' turn to go

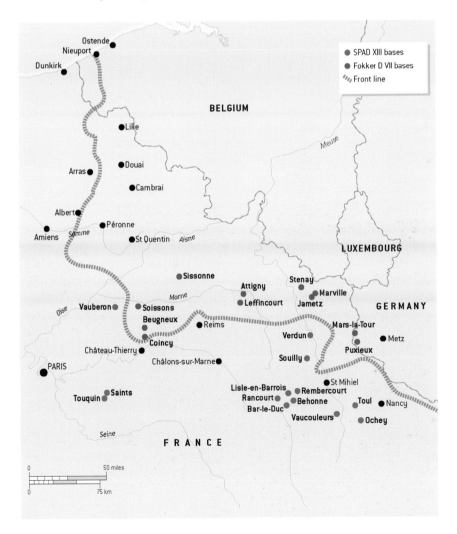

Throughout the German and Allied offensives of 1918, both sides shifted their fighter groups or squadrons to whichever front seemed most critical. By October the Americans were facing both JG II, based at Stenay, and Marville-based JG I – the 'Flying Circus' – over the Meuse-Argonne.

In this rare view, SPAD XIIIs of the 103rd Aero Sqn sit in front of a typical hangar at Vaucouleurs aerodrome in September 1918. Note the French rudder stripes on aeroplane No. 12 in the foreground. (Livingston Irving album via Jon Guttman)

onto the offensive once more, starting with the French army that same day, followed by the British along the Somme on 8 August and the Americans at St Mihiel on 12 September.

Much needed improvements in the reliability of the Hispano-Suiza 8B allowed the SPAD XIII to proliferate throughout the French air service, and by September the USAS also boasted three operational pursuit groups of four squadrons each, fully equipped with SPAD XIIIs.

Although rapidly growing numbers of Fokker D VIIs equipped the *Jagdgeschwader*, and they were slowly finding their way into army *Jastas* and naval *Marine Feld Jastas* too, their tactical deployment had reverted to the situation prior to Operation *Michael*. Units were now shifting from one base to another to concentrate against whichever Allied offensive seemed most threatening at the moment.

Yet in spite of the flagging spirits permeating the German army, the D VII pilots retained faith in their aeroplanes, and a dogged determination to do their part in making the Allies pay dearly for every gain either on the ground or in the air. Given the overwhelming and still growing preponderance of aircraft swelling the Allied ranks, however, the D VII pilots could do little more than delay their country's ultimate, inevitable defeat.

THE COMBATANTS

Aéronautique Française

French fighter pilot training was not exactly uniform, with literally two schools for learning the fundamentals of flight. SPAD pilot André Martenot de Cordoux, an infantryman who was accepted into the Aéronautique Française on 15 August 1915, described the primary training he received, with a passing reference to the other method:

> I started my training at the school at Pau, in 25hp and 45hp 'Penguins'. The Penguin was a Blériot aeroplane with its wings cut short. It was not truly an aeroplane for it only hopped a few metres in the air. With a 45hp motor you could bounce about 20 metres, but not for long. You simply rolled about the field in them. The instructor, or *moniteur*, would let you go on your way across the field, then turn and come back. The *moniteur* would estimate how much control you exercised. You went strictly solo – that was to build confidence in a pilot, as it simulated lone flight. We had a nice large field, so no one would be in the way.
>
> Then it was onto 100hp Blériots, learning to fly in a circle. You would do a circuit of 150 kilometres during the final test for your brevet, or flying certificate. We had several accidents every week – some killed, some injured. For my own part, I never had a mishap in training. On 26 December 1915 I earned my military pilot's brevet.
>
> There was, by the way, another training field at Avord that used two-

Sous-Lt André Martenot de Cordoux, who scored six to eight victories in a Caudron G 4, a Nieuport 24 and SPAD VIIs and XIIIs, sports a silver pin of SPA94's 'La Morte Qui Fauche' marking, which he claimed to have conceived. (SHAA B92.4178)

ANDRÉ MARTENOT DE CORDOUX
AS AUX HUIT VICTOIRES OFFICIELLES

GEORGES FÉLIX MADON

Born in Bizerte, Tunisia, on 28 July 1892, Georges Félix Madon received his civil pilot's license on 7 June 1911 and joined the French army as an engineer on 12 March 1912. On 1 January 1913 he transferred to aviation, and after training at Avord obtained military pilot's brevet No 231. Madon was a caporal flying Blériots with Bl30 when war broke out, later becoming a sergent and transitioning to Maurice Farmans. On 5 July 1915 he and his mechanic became lost in bad weather and landed in neutral Switzerland. After one failure, Madon succeeded in escaping from Swiss internment on 27 December, only to be 'rewarded' by the French authorities with 60 days' confinement for blundering into the airspace of their neutral neighbour in the first place!

After serving in MF218, Madon asked to become a chasse pilot, and following training at Pau and Cazaux he was assigned to N38 on 1 September 1916. He soon showed his mettle, downing a Fokker E III on 28 September, followed by two more on 9 and 17 November, for which he received the Médaille Militaire. After despatching an LVG on 10 December, Madon was promoted to adjutant on the 16th. On 5 May 1917, the day after scoring his tenth victory, he was made a Chevalier de la Légion d'Honneur.

Wounded in action on 2 July, Madon resumed his scoring on 18 August, and on 24 March 1918 – now a lieutenant – he was put in command of SPA38. Although his personal thistle insignia had evolved into a squadron pennant, Madon, as its leader, chose to identify himself to his pilots in the same way that Manfred von Richthofen had – by painting the fuselage of his SPAD XIII, and a cannon-equipped SPAD XII, red. Madon's first credited Fokker came on 12 June 1918, and the 'scouts' downed by him on 17 July were undoubtedly D VIIs, as were the definite D VIIs he downed on 31 July and 11 August and the 'scout' that became his 41st, and last, official victim on 3 September.

In addition to his official tally, which made him the fourth-ranking French ace, Madon was reported to have scored so many uncredited victories that had he been in the RAF or the USAS, his score would have reached 100! Whenever told that a claim could not be confirmed by his

air arm's relatively strict standards, however, Madon would typically dismiss the matter, casually remarking 'the Boches know their losses'.

Madon was also fondly remembered by those he mentored, as he was always keen to share his techniques with others. André Martenot de Cordoux of N94, who had previously served alongside Madon, remarked on the occasion of his second victory, a Rumpler C IV on 25 July 1917, 'I remembered what Madon had told me about how to attack a bi-place – keep out of the line of fire of his rear gun. I approached from slightly below, zig-zagging from side to side until I was ready to take aim, then I fired from behind and below'.

Given the temporary rank of capitaine on the last day of the war, Madon was made an Officier de la Légion d'Honneur on 25 November, by which time he also held the Croix de Guerre with 17 palms and one bronze star. Having survivied the war, Madon perished on 11 November 1924 in a flying accident in Tunis during a celebration of the Armistice and the inauguration of a statue to prewar and early war hero Roland Garros.

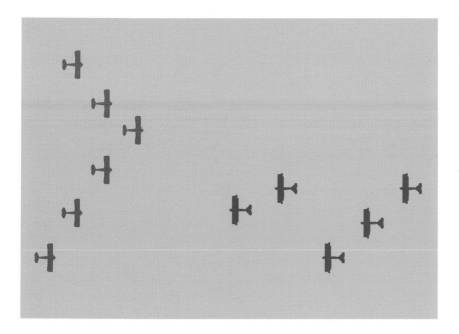

seater Caudrons for dual-control training for those who wanted an alternate means to the 'Blériot' method at Pau.

After you took the test circuit, the commandant, observing the steadiness and skill of the student, would choose the pilot for his role. The pilot was then trained further on more advanced aircraft – Nieuports for scout pilots, Voisin pushers for bomber training and the Caudron or Farman for reconnaissance training. I was assigned to the Caudrons.

On 7 February 1916, Martenot left Avord for the Groupe Division d'Entrainement (GDE) at Plessis-Belleville, where he continued training until assigned to operational

Commandant Edouard Duseigneur, commander of Groupe de Combat 11 comprising SPA12, 31, 57 and 154, stands before his Blériot-built SPAD XIII. The griffin emblem was his own personal marking. (SHAA B83.3265)

43

escadrille C28 on 9 April 1916. Flying a twin-engined Caudron G 4, Cpl Martenot and his observer-gunner Soldat de 2e Classe Claude Martin shot down an LVG on 20 May. Badly wounded during the fight, Martenot left the hospital in February 1917 with his right leg seven centimetres shorter than his left.

In spite of this handicap, he underwent aerial gunnery and flight training in single-seaters, then served in interceptor détachement N513 of the Groupe de Protection outside Paris, also flying reconnaissance missions on detached duty with C56 and N38. The latter *escadrille's* distinguished airmen included Sous-Lt Georges Madon, who was the fourth-ranking French ace with 41 victories. More importantly, Madon was an outstanding mentor whose tutelage helped Martenot and N38 LFC volunteer David Putnam 'make ace' in their own right.

After being wounded in the arm during combat and injured further in the subsequent crash landing, Martenot returned to find N513, along with Détachements N512 and N514, merged into new fighter escadrille N94 on 14 May 1917. He spent the rest of the war with that outfit flying Nieuport 24s, SPAD VIIs and XIIIs, and increasing his tally to at least six and possibly as many as eight victories.

The basic French and American element within the squadron usually comprised three aeroplanes in V formation, which by 1918 had been expanded to a flight of six to nine. Martenot described his escadrille SPA94 as usually operating in two flights, whereas the American pursuit squadrons, like the British, always had three.

An interesting – and, in retrospect, advanced – alternative to the usual V-shaped element most common for SPADs was described by Sous-Lt Edwin C. Parsons, a former member of N124 'Lafayette' who transferred to the famous SPA3 *'Les*

Officers and ground personnel of the 103rd Aero Sqn with a SPAD XIII at Vaucouleurs in September 1918. Identified from second left are 1Lts Martin F. McQuiken, Lawrence E. Cauffman, G. DeFreest Larner, Frank O'D. Hunter, Hugo A. Kenyon and Livingston Irving. (Livingston Irving album via Jon Guttman)

Cigognes' in February 1918. Parsons said he and comrade Adj Jean Denneulin devised a 'hunter-killer technique' that involved the latter flying 50 metres above and 50 metres to the left or right of Parsons. 'I never had to look – he was always there', Parsons recalled. 'If he spotted enemy aeroplanes that might endanger us, he'd sweep down waggling his wings and pointing to the danger zone. If I spotted our quarry, I'd waggle and we'd go into the attack.'

This flexible tactic for mutual support, first employed to shoot down a two-seater on 16 May and subsequently to score two more joint victories, bears a remarkable resemblance to the basic Rotte and Vierfinger concepts credited to German ace Werner Mölders during the Spanish Civil War almost 20 years later.

Former Lafayette Flying Corps ace 1Lt David E. Putnam was a flight leader in the 139th Aero Sqn with 13 accredited victories to his name when he was killed by Ltn Georg von Hantelmann of Jasta 15 on 12 September 1918. Both men were just 19 at the time. (Jack Eder Collection via Jon Guttman)

FRANK O'DRISCOLL HUNTER

Born in Savannah, Georgia, on 8 December 1894, Frank O'Driscoll Hunter graduated from the Hotchkiss School in 1913 and joined the Aviation Section of the US Army Signal Corps in 1917. After training in the United States and France, he was assigned to the 94th Aero Sqn on 22 May 1918, but reassigned to the 103rd Aero Sqn a week later. There, he acquired the nickname 'Monk', which he apparently liked, because his SPAD XIII sported a small personal marking in the form of a monkey below the cockpit.

Hunter's first victory was over a two-seater near Mount Kemmel on 2 June, but he did not score again until 13 September, when he and 1Lt Gorman DeFreest Larner, his flight leader who had two previous victories as an LFC member with SPA86, shared in downing a Fokker D VII. '"Monk" Hunter was my deputy flight commander, and the most courageous and aggressive flier in the 103rd while I was there', Larner recalled. 'It would do me an injustice to put me in the same class with "Monk" Hunter, who was so much my superior as a fighter boy. He was a true dare-devil.'

Coming fully into his stride, Hunter downed two D VIIs near Verneville on 17 September, two more near Ligny-devant-Dun on 4 October and another Fokker at Banthéville two days later. He and another LFC veteran, 1Lt William T. Ponder, downed a Halbertadt two-seater over La Croix aux Bois on 19 October, and four days later Hunter and 1Lt Percy R. Pyne bagged a D VII near Dun-sur-

Meuse, bringing the ace's total to nine, seven of which were Fokkers.

By the end of the war Hunter had received the DSC with four Oak Leaf Clusters and the French Légion d'Honneur. Remaining in the Army Air Corps, he did some early mail flying, had to parachute from his aeroplane three times – in 1925, 1926 and 1933 – and rose in rank to major in 1936 and colonel in December 1941. He served for a time as air attaché to London, and during World War II Maj Gen Hunter was in charge of the Eighth Air Force's VIII Fighter Command. He retired from the USAAF on 31 March 1946, and his life ended where it started, in Savannah, on 25 June 1982.

In January 1918, the French expanded further on their 1916 concept of the *groupe de combat* or its German equivalent, the *Jagdgeschwader*, as a means of achieving local air superiority. Escadre de Combat 1, commanded by the veteran Chef de Bataillon Victor Menard, combined three such *groupes*, GC15 (SPA37, 81, 93 and 97), GC18 (SPA48, 94, 153 and 155) and GC19 (SPA73, 85, 95 and 96).

With pilots being unable to communicate with each other when in the air beyond the use of flare guns, hand gestures and wing waggling, any coordinated effort by the groups, squadrons and wings had to be decided upon prior to the mission commencing. Such planning was heavily dependent on everyone reaching the rendezvous point on time. The *escadre* concept, which gave the French a single unified command that could move 12 fighter squadrons to whichever sector required their services, was soon put to the test.

USAS

American SPAD pilots were products of a wide variety of training and experience. Some started at home on docile two-seat Curtiss JN-4s, followed by single-seat Thomas-Morse S 4C or Standard E 1 fighter trainers. Others learned in France at one or more of the 12 training aerodromes the USAS established in Issoudun, hoping that an accident would not curtail their careers prematurely at 'Field 13' – the adjacent cemetery. Some trained in Britain and a few in Foggia, Italy, before being transferred to France for fighter conversion onto Nieuports and SPADs.

The newly enlisted USAS pilots were fortunate in having their ranks leavened with a cadre of veterans transferred in from French service with the LFC or from Britain's RFC. Had it not been for the experience imparted by squadron leaders like Capt Charles J. Biddle, operations officers such as Maj G. Raoul Lufbery or flight leaders like 1Lt David Putnam, the casualties suffered by the high-spirited, but often overconfident, neophytes would have been far greater. Besides the Lafayette volunteers, scores of USAS pilots were farmed out to French *escadrilles* through the GDE, filling out their attrited ranks and gaining invaluable combat experience until enough SPADs were available for their own units.

Leighton Brewer, who was one of only five pilots to serve in the 13th Aero Sqn from start to finish, completed his flight training at Issoudun on 1 May, but until enough SPADs arrived to equip his fighter outfit, he and several colleagues volunteered to fly reconnaissance missions in Sopwith 1A2s and Salmson 2A2s with the 90th Aero Sqn, based at Ourches. At the end of June he and 1Lt Harry B. Freeman were ordered to the 13th, commanded by Capt Biddle, who already had two victories to his credit while flying in N73 and with the 103rd Aero Sqn.

Biddle was encouraged by the high level of skill and morale exhibited by most of his pilots, but past experience left him all too aware of the quality of the opposition, and the penchant of German *Jagdstaffeln* to pounce on any SPAD pilot cocky enough to venture off on his own. Biddle wrote home of how he strove to impress the importance of team effort and 'discouraging the great tendency for one man to try to dash off by himself and be a hero at the expense of the whole', adding that, 'Any man who leaves a patrol for such a purpose will be put on the ground for a couple of weeks and confined to camp, and if he repeats the performance I shall send him to the rear'.

Leighton Brewer recalled his experiences upon reaching the 13th Aero Sqn:

> We initially had six men to a flight, but during the first or second week in August they added a seventh. The Flight Commander always led his flight, but the rest of us flew different positions in it in order to gain experience. When we patrolled with an odd number of aeroplanes, we flew in a V, and when we had an even number, the extra man flew a little above the V, closing its rear.
>
> We never operated on a scale larger than a squadron. Frequently, the whole group was out at the same time, but operating at different levels.
>
> We used to take off whenever we were ready, or if everyone was ready, at the same time

Ltn Gustav Frädrich of Jasta 72s, based at Bergnicourt aerodrome in July 1918, sports a Heinecke parachute, which was unreliable but often proved to be more of a lifesaver than the Allied pilots' issuance of no parachutes at all. (Greg VanWyngarden)

in order of side numbers. We would meet at 1,000 metres over some designated spot, assemble the formation and then start climbing as we approached the lines. Most of our flights were high ones, 3,500 or 5,000 metres, except when we were strafing infantry, or whenever we had low clouds.

Actually, I flew on the highest level patrol flown by the USAS in World War I. Our flight had gone out on 7 September, with Freeman leading. We sighted a group of German aeroplanes on their side of the lines at about 5,000 metres and started climbing to get above them. We climbed, and they climbed, until we got up to 21,500ft and they couldn't quite make it. So, we crossed over and hopped them. Didn't miss oxygen much, but I felt very bloated. That's another thing – you couldn't eat too much breakfast before a high patrol or you'd swell up a lot.'

LUFTSTREITSKRÄFTE

German fighter pilots had often served in reconnaissance or bombing units before requesting transfer to, or being seconded due to displays of an aggressive nature for training at, one of the two German fighter schools. Born in 1897, Alfred Wenz had enlisted in the infantry – and was wounded – in 1914, at age 16. 'I later became a flyer by first attending a single-seater fighter school at Valenciennes, before moving to Braunschweig and the pilot replacement centre, where I was eventually sent to a two-seater squadron for a few weeks', he explained. 'Later I was assigned to Jagdstaffel 11 of the Richthofen Jagdgeschwader'.

Ltn Wenz was credited with five victories, but he is best known for what occurred on 10 August 1918. 'Soon after shooting down an English aeroplane over the River Somme at about 12,000ft', he wrote, 'I collided with my comrade, Oblt Löwenhardt. It was necessary that we both take to our parachutes. Mine opened. His did not. That was a great misfortune'.

That incident highlighted the most marked difference between German and Allied airmen in 1918. Uffz Otto Heinecke, a groundcrewman in Flieger Abteilung 23, had devised a more compact parachute pack to give pilots the same option of abandoning a doomed aeroplane that had already been afforded balloon observers by the bulkier Paulus parachutes since the war began. When the necessity arose, the airman jumped from the aeroplane and a static line attached to a harness around his shoulder and legs would pull the parachute pack clear of the empennage before a second static line, secured inside the cockpit, extricated the canopy from the pack.

Parachuting from aircraft had been done since 1911, and practical 'chutes such as Heinecke's had in fact been conceived as early as 1916. The Germans had issued a few for experimental use in 1917, but their operational employment was delayed by high-ranking officers on both sides, who debated whether they would encourage aircrews to abandon aeroplanes that could be ridden to the ground, or even undermine their aggressiveness in the air. The Luftstreistkräfte, heavily outnumbered even as Germany launched the *Kaiserschlacht*, was the first to declare such objections as utter nonsense, and the consequent loss of trained airmen whose lives might otherwise be saved to be a luxury it could ill afford.

The first Heinecke parachutes began arriving at *Jagdstaffeln* in April 1918 – at about the same time as the first Fokker D VIIs were making their way to JG I.

The parachutes got off to a shaky start. Some pilots, including Manfred von Richthofen, doubted their reliability as being worth the 15 kilograms they added to their fighters' weight. Their early use seemed to justify the scepticism, as an alarming one-third of the first 70 airmen to bale out were killed, either because their parachutes caught on the empennage of their aeroplanes, or because the harnesses gave way under the stress of a body suddenly jerked out of free fall at 80mph.

The latter problem was addressed in the late summer of 1918 by the adoption of reinforced harnesses with wider leg straps that distributed the weight better. That resulted in a noticeable improvement in the parachutes' reliability, and an encouragingly higher survival rate. As with the Fokker D VII, however, even as they gained acceptance there were never enough parachutes to go around. Pilots often had to share with their *Jasta* mates, and repair damaged or partially burned parachutes for re-use.

Still, at least the Germans had a choice toward survival in mid to late 1918. The RAF finally ordered that parachutes be issued to its single-seat squadrons on 16 September 1918. The French and Americans did not allow their pilots to use them at all before the armistice.

Although German fighter tactics were founded on the Boelcke Dicta, how each *Jasta* carried out those basic principles varied with the unit commander's policy. Some *Staffelführer* were cautious – and in the case of those leading newly formed *Amerika-Programm* units, the caution was justified. Others exuded an aggressive confidence that rubbed off on the pilots, or was imposed directly upon them.

When Uffz Willi Gabriel, a Halberstadt CL II ground attack pilot with Schutzstaffel 15, transferred to JG I on 19 May 1918, he recalled the following greeting from its commander, Hptm Wilhelm Reinhard:

> We know that you can fly, but it is of no use coming here to rest on your laurels. This is no rest-camp. If you have no confirmed victory within four weeks you may remove yourself back to your unit. You are posted to Jasta 11.

Gabriel duly brought down a DH 9 four days later. His final tally of 11 included four in one day.

Besides leading the *Geschwader* en masse, Reinhard (like Manfred von Richthofen before him) allowed pilots to fly lone sorties under the right circumstances – a policy that Gabriel, for one, liked. After Reinhard's death while test-flying a Dornier D I prototype on 3 July, however, Oblt Hermann Göring was assigned command of JG I, and he forbade lone patrolling.

'In 1918', Wenz recalled, 'it was necessary to take off on patrols three to five times a day, which meant that daily we had flyers who were killed, wounded or missing in action. In the last months of the war, we would have 20 or 30 aircraft in the air at one time, and it was necessary that we combat the American, English or French groups of 100 to 120 aeroplanes'.

These Fokker D VIIs, bearing the red and white livery and raven emblems of Ltn August Rabe's Jasta 18, have been neatly lined up for inspection by visiting chief of the Luftstreitskräfte, Gen Ltn Ernst Wilhelm von Hoeppner. (Greg VanWyngarden)

GEORG VON HANTELMANN

Like the prototypical Prussian villain for a Hollywood film like *Hell's Angels*, Georg von Hantelmann used a skull and crossbones as a personal marking and had a prodigious talent for killing off Allied heroes. He was also one of the youngest German aces, and their most successful destroyer of SPAD XIIIs, with no fewer than 15 figuring among his 25 victories – all made possible by flying the Fokker D VII.

Born on 9 October 1898, von Hantelmann joined the German Army in 1916, and on 15 June 1917 was commissioned as a *Leutnant* in Hussar Regiment Nr 17 – the 'Death's Head Hussars' from whose emblem he derived his later aeroplane marking. Soon transferring to the air service, he began training at Flieger Erstaz Abteilung 9 on 20 September, followed by Jastaschule at Valenciennes. Assigned to Jasta 18 on 6 February, von Hantelmann was part of the unit's wholesale exchange with Jasta 15 on 18 March.

He made his first SPAD XIII claim on 29 May 1918, although it remained unconfirmed, but on 6 June he downed a DH 4 of No. 27 Sqn, followed by credited victories over a SPAD and a Sopwith Camel four days later.

Von Hantelmann's score reached six on 17 August, but rose spectacularly after JG II began operations against the Americans over St Mihiel. On 12 September he killed 1Lt David E. Putnam, an LFC veteran of N156 and SPA38, and flight leader in the 139th Aero Sqn with 13 accredited victories.

Von Hantelmann scored a triple victory over a DH 4 and two SPAD XIIIs on 14 September. Then, on the 16th, Sous-Lt Maurice Boyau of SPA77, former captain of the French rugby team and victor over 34 aircraft and balloons, was leading Cpl René Walk, Asp Henri Cessieux and LFC Cpl Edward C. Corsi on a mission to eliminate a kite balloon at Harville. Boyau and Cessieux set the 'gasbag' alight, but then the French SPAD XIII pilots were jumped by seven Fokkers of Jasta 15.

Corsi later recalled, 'A dogfight ensued. I saw one German go down. As they broke off I saw a SPAD on my right headed home. I flew with him back to the field. It was Cessieux. He had a bad leg wound and just about made it. My aeroplane had been hit many times. Boyau never

returned, and though an extensive search was made, his body was never found'.

After evading his first assailant, Boyau had dived under the burning balloon and tried to drive a Fokker off Walk's tail – only to be hit by either another fighter or by ground fire. Boyau fell in flames, his demise credited to von Hantelmann. His sacrifice had not been entirely in vain, however, for Walk, though credited to Vzfw Gustav Klaudat, made it to Allied lines before force-landing his damaged SPAD.

On 18 September von Hantelmann killed 1Lt Joseph F. Wehner, famed sidekick of leading American balloon buster 2Lt Frank Luke of the 27th Aero Sqn – his third kill over an ace in just a week. Von Hantelmann's 20th (yet another SPAD XIII) fell on his 20th birthday. A SPAD on 4 November brought his total to 25, but while he was awarded the Iron Cross 1st and 2nd Class, as well as the Knight's Cross of the Royal Hohenzollern House Order on 21 October, the Kaiser's abdication denied him receipt of the coveted Orden Pour le Mérite.

After the war, Georg von Hantelmann retired to his family estate in East Prussia, only to be slain in an armed altercation with Polish poachers on 7 September 1924.

COMBAT

The series of Allied offensives from mid-July to the armistice were replete with aerial clashes between SPAD XIIIs and Fokker D VIIs, many of them well documented by unit records, citations for awards, in the participants' personal logs or letters, or all of the above. Generally, they involved French or American units venturing into German territory and having to fight their way back, but there were occasional German forays over the lines to pursue a fleeing reconnaissance aeroplane, strafe Allied troops or have a go at an especially troublesome Allied balloon.

One French squadron that had had particularly bad luck against the Fokkers was SPA159. Between its formation on 16 January 1918 and late July, the *escadrille* had not scored a single confirmed victory, while losing 13 pilots killed or taken prisoner. That included its commander, Lt Georges Mazimann, killed in a SPAD VII by Oblt Bruno Loerzer of Jagdgeschwader III on 20 July.

By then, SPA159 was getting SPAD XIIIs, but just as important as the new aircraft was its new leader. On the 29th, Lt Henri Hay de Slade was transferred from SPA86 to take command, with Sous-Lt Louis Risacher, who had previously scored two victories in SPA3, assigned as his deputy. 'Slade was a nice companion', Risacher recalled. 'The rest were young pilots who knew nothing about the job. I had to teach them everything. Everything.' Slade, then credited with 11 victories, was equally at a loss as to what to do to reverse the unit's fortunes:

I'd been something of a loner before, and did not know how to impart my techniques to others. But something had to be done, so I had my SPAD XIII painted all over with prominent red stripes down the fuselage, and before taking the men up on patrol I told them that in the event of combat to stay up and watch what I did. I knew that the red stripes would make it easy for them to recognise me in the most confused dogfight.

Sure enough, we came upon an enemy formation, and I dived into them, deliberately going through all my standard manoeuvres in the course of the fight, during which I managed to shoot down one of my adversaries. After a few such 'lessons', I gradually let the others join me in combat to apply what they had seen, and it must have worked because from then on SPA159 started taking a toll of the enemy, while its losses markedly decreased.

On 11 August, Sgt Georges Priollaud, an experienced transferee from SPA65, claimed SPA159's first confirmed victory. Slade resumed his scoring three days later, ultimately bringing his own tally up to 19, including two balloons (one shared with LFC Sgt Edwin Bradley Fairchild) on 10 October.

Risacher shot down two German fighters over the Forêt de St Gobain on 31 August and scored his fifth over a D VII on 18 October:

I had a young pilot with me, and that absurd fellow saw five or six Fokker D VIIs below us. I'd seen them, of course, but I was not in position to attack. But as soon as he saw them he attacked, so I had to save him. That's why I dove myself to let him get away, but I had all the Huns behind me and above me, and they shot at me for five to ten minutes. Suddenly, I saw a SPAD coming in, shooting. The Germans saw the source of the attack – one German passed to my left with the SPAD on his tail. The SPAD shot him and he fell to pieces. It was Claude Haegelen of SPA100.

At the very same moment a second SPAD – I knew it was an American aeroplane by his cockades – coming in at full speed took on another Hun and shot him to pieces. I said 'God save America!', and at that moment I put speed to my old aeroplane and took a third D VII in a loop. He looked behind at me and then fell to pieces, crashing to earth. The others went away.'

SPAD XIIIs of the hitherto-hapless SPA159 at Lormaison aerodrome in August 1918. The red-striped machine was flown by the newly appointed commander, Lt Henry Hay de Slade, while aeroplane No. 2, with what seems to be a red vertical stabiliser, was probably flown by his deputy, Lt Louis Risacher. (SHAA B76.613)

Risacher's Yankee benefactor seems to have been 1Lt Chester E. Wright of the 93rd Aero Sqn, who scored his fourth victory over Banthéville at 1100 hrs that day – and whose victim may have been Ltn d R Erich Klink of Jasta 68, killed in that location. Wright would down two more Fokkers that afternoon. Haegelen's opponent went down west of Landres St Georges for his 21st victory. Risacher's fifth, which fell over Buzancy, was also the 12th, and final, success for SPA159.

Although Edwin Fairchild was the only original member to make a contribution to SPA159's belated victory list, Slade's leadership by example did significantly reduce its casualties. On 2 September he claimed a scout over Terny-Sorny, and though Sous-Lt René d'Aux was wounded – and possibly credited to Flg Eyssler of Jasta 66 – he did not leave the fight until the enemy disengaged. On 3 October SPA159's Cpl Raymond Desouches was lost in a SPAD VII, probably becoming the tenth victim of Vzfw Dietrich Averes of Jasta 81. MdL Marcel Granger and his SPAD XIII went missing on the 21st, probably falling to the guns of Ltn von Hantelmann of Jasta 15, and two days later 'Brad' Fairchild became the *escadrille*'s last casualty, although he lived to add his testimony to the hazards of fighting the D VII:

I was shot down by a Fokker, so I can tell you they were wonderful. Around Marcq, I led a patrol against some 'cold meat'. I attacked him and holed his wings, but he

SPAD XIII FUSELAGE GUNS

Most SPAD XIIIs were armed with two 0.303-in Vickers machine guns, each firing 400 rounds, using mechanical interruptor gear developed by Marc Birkigt for his Hispano-Suiza engines. Some American SPADs carried two 0.30-cal Marlin machine guns instead of the twin Vickers.

outmanoeuvred me. I tried to pass under him so as to let the others hop him. I looked up to see the other four SPADs heading home with eight Fokkers onto them. He put a bullet through my reserve tank and gas blew in my face. I heard a 'crash', breaking my stick, and I went down into a spin. I came down in the trees. It knocked me out, and I was in hospital for a couple of days. I was very fortunate.

Fairchild's opponent, Jasta 11's Ltn Friedrich Noltenius, wrote his own recollection of the encounter that showed both how wrong the American was in regarding him as 'cold meat', and just how fortunate his 17th confirmed victim had been:

I saw four SPADs arrive from the north. I turned back in order not to be cut off, and met them at the front. Immediately I attacked the lowest one. He spun down and I went after him without the others intervening. We finally romped around at an altitude of just 50 metres. Whilst in a turn, I hit him in the fuel tank. Then both my guns jammed completely and I had to break off because I saw the other three SPADs come down, and without ammunition, I was unable to fight it out with them.'

USAS SPAD XIIIs INTO ACTION

While the critical Third Battle of the Marne was taking place, the American 2nd and

FOKKER D VII FUSELAGE GUNS

The Fokker D VII was armed with two 7.92mm LMG 08/15 machine guns, combined with Anthony Fokker's proven *Zentralsteuerung* (centralised control) cam-activated interruptor gear. The D VII carried a total of 1,000 rounds of ammunition.

3rd Pursuit Groups were being organised in the relatively quiet Toul sector in preparation for Gen Pershing's planned St Mihiel offensive. This included the veteran 103rd Aero Sqn, which arrived in late June to find the local *Amerika-Programm Jastas* 64w and 65 significantly bolstered by the arrival of Jasta 18 – the first unit in the sector fully equipped with Fokker D VIIs. By August Jastas 64w and 65 were replacing their Albatros and Pfalz scouts with D VIIs as well.

The 103rd's first clash with a D VII occurred during a mid-morning patrol on 1 August, when 1Lt Edgar G. Tobin attacked one with a black fuselage and red tail at an altitude of 1,500 metres. After firing 75 rounds at it, he saw it fall off in a vrille. This went rightly unconfirmed, but at 2010 hrs on the 10th, Tobin took on another Fokker at an altitude of 4,500 metres and, after firing 75 rounds, saw it fall out of control to crash near Thiaucourt. This was credited as Tobin's fourth victory (of an eventual six), and Jasta 64w recorded the loss of Flg Herbert Koch, killed at Pont-á-Mousson.

Mid-August saw the return of the 1st Pursuit Group to the sector from its ordeal around Château-Thierry.

In the less-seasoned 13th Aero Sqn of the 2nd Pursuit Group, Capt Biddle was encouraged by the high level of skill and general morale of most of his pilots, but he tried to stress the importance of team effort and 'discouraged the great tendency for one man to try to dash off by himself and be a hero at the expense of the whole', adding that 'any man who leaves a patrol for such a purpose will be put on the ground for a couple of weeks and confined to camp, and if he repeats the performance I shall send him to the rear'.

The youngest of the 2nd Pursuit Group's squadrons, the 22nd, opened its account when 1Lt A. Raymond Brooks downed a Rumpler over Armacourt on 2 September. Two days later, Brooks was leading 1Lts Frank B. Tyndall and Clinton Jones Jr on patrol when they saw the 10th Balloon Company's 'gasbag' go up in flames. Giving chase to its attacker, the trio drove the Fokker D VII down in German lines, wounding Swiss pilot Uffz Albert Bader of Jasta 64w.

The St Mihiel push commenced on 12 September, with Pershing directing 665,000 troops in 19 divisions, backed by 3,220 guns and 267 tanks, to clear the salient of the ten divisions of Gen Max von Gallwitz's Armee Gruppe C. Aware of their precarious situation, the Germans were caught in the act of withdrawing, resulting in the capture of some 15,000 troops and 257 guns within six days at a cost of 7,000 Allied casualties – one-third of what the Army Medical Corps had anticipated.

In the air, Brig Gen William Mitchell commanded 1,476 aircraft (mostly American and French, but including three Italian Caproni bomber squadrons). Additional voluntary support was lent by the nine British bomber squadrons of Maj Gen Hugh Trenchard's Independent Force. Besides Jastas 18, 64w and 65, however, the Germans had transferred JG II (under Oblt Oskar von Bönigk, and comprising Jastas 12, 13, 15 and 19) into the sector. The Fokker pilots still faced a hopeless task challenging the Allies' numerical supremacy, but they inflicted a heavy toll on the Americans nevertheless.

Rain and thunderstorms marred the offensive's first day, but both sides flew sorties whenever they could. At 1020 hrs 1Lt Leslie J. Rummell of the 93rd Aero Sqn claimed a Fokker D VII over Thiaucourt, but then became lost in a cloud, ran out of fuel and

had to crash-land. Nearby, his squadronmate 1Lt Charles Rudolph D'Olive fired 25 to 30 rounds at a Fokker over Vieville-en-Haye, and claimed to have seen the German go down in a steep spin when a magneto quit and he had to retire.

While those future aces were opening their accounts, 1Lt David Putnam of the 139th Aero Sqn was closing his. At 1830 hrs he engaged eight Fokker D VIIs and downed one for his 13th official victory. On his way home, he saw seven more Fokkers attacking a Breguet 14 over Limey and plunged into the enemy formation. His intervention saved the two-seater, but he was struck twice in the heart and came down in a poppy field. Putnam and the man credited with shooting him down, Ltn Georg von Hantelmann of Jasta 15, were the same age – 19.

The weather improved on 13 September, heralding several days of intense combat. At 0900 hrs on the 14th, Jasta 18 hit the 13th Aero Sqn over Thiaucourt, with Ltn Hans Müller claiming three SPADs and Lts Günther von Büren and Heinz Küstner downing one each in the next 15 minutes. A survivor of this one-sided clash was 1Lt Leighton Brewer, who recalled:

On the 14th we were given a low patrol, at a height of 2,500 metres. We were flying this when we were attacked by a group of red-nosed Fokkers. We lost four aeroplanes within one minute! I was flying between a couple of men who were shot down, but I only got one bullet in the tail of my aeroplane. The first indication I had that enemy aircraft were

Ltn Günther von Büren of Jasta 18 was credited with destroying a SPAD of the 13th Aero Sqn for his second victory on 14 September 1918, although he was himself brought down wounded by the combined fire of three other 'Grim Reapers' just minutes later. (Greg VanWyngarden)

nearby was when I saw a red Fokker with a white fuselage standing on its nose and spraying the fellow behind me with bullets. Two Fokkers with red wings and noses and white fuselages dived on us, and they shot down the men on either side of me. 1Lts Charlie Drew, George Kull, Buck Freeman and 'Steve' Brody were all lost. Drew was very badly wounded, Kull was killed and the other two were prisoners.

1Lt Charles W. Drew was taken prisoner – later to have his wounded leg amputated – as were 1Lt Alton A. Brody and 1Lt Harry B. Freeman, but 1Lt George R. Kull was killed. Two Fokkers were jointly credited to 1Lts Robert H. Stiles, Gerald D. Stivers and Murray K. Guthrie, but Jasta 18's only casualty was von Büren, who was wounded. Grieving over his losses, Capt Biddle attributed them to the fact that in spite of his relentless warnings, 'the new men will get carried away with themselves in a combat and go too strong'.

One of many pilots who could testify to the SPAD XIII's durability that morning was 1Lt Sumner Sewell of the 95th Aero Sqn. Jumped at the tail end of his formation by JG II's CO, Oblt von Boenigk, Sewell dropped out with a burning fuel tank. Going into a power dive in an attempt to keep the flames away from his cockpit, he succeeded in blowing them out and crash-landed in Allied lines. Moments after he crawled from the charred wreckage, an object brushed Sewell's elbow and thumped down at his feet. It was the wheel of his aeroplane, which had come off during his dive!

That afternoon Capt Ray C. Bridgman, commander of the 22nd Aero Sqn, led 'C' Flight as escorts for a Salmson 2A2 on a reconnaissance mission at 1300 hrs. When the six Americans arrived at the rendezvous point at Mars-la-Tour, however, all they found were three stepped formations of five, six and twelve Fokkers! The latter, uppermost, D VIIs, sporting the blue fuselages and red cowls of Jasta 15, descended on the SPADs. 1Lt Brooks, serving as deputy in the first-left position, climbed to engage the Germans, and ended up fighting eight of them. Four others fell upon the rest of the flight.

Brooks saw 1Lt Philip E. Hassinger shot down in flames. Over the next ten minutes, he took on eight of the Fokkers in an effort to cover the retirement of his remaining comrades, claiming to have shot down two of his antagonists and damaged two others, before force landing in Allied

Ltn Franz Büchner, CO of Jasta 13, celebrates his 30th victory before his OAW-built Fokker D VII on 18 September 1918. No fewer than 13 of his final 40-aeroplane tally were French or American SPAD XIIIs. (Greg VanWyngarden)

lines. Although miraculously unhurt, he later said that he was 'all in' in tears over Hassinger's death, and was convinced that his entire flight had been wiped out. Brooks, who insisted upon sharing the credit for his two confirmed victories with Hassinger, was awarded the DSC.

Arthur Kimber, who had been attached to SPA85 before joining the 22nd, was in the left rear of the formation 'to bring up the tail and cover the others', and he subsequently described what happened to the rest of 'C' Flight during Brooks' epic struggle:

About four of the red-nosed, blue-bodied machines jumped on me. They had height and were in the sun, and all I could do was wriggle. At that moment I looked below and saw that five or six other Fokkers had come up and were attacking the rest of the patrol. In a dogfight like that, it soon develops into each man for himself, and the devil takes the hindmost. Well, I was the hindmost! But at the same time I didn't like the idea of being easy meat for the devil Huns. We were about 5,200 metres high and about ten kilometres behind the Boche lines.

I watched my tail like a cat and saw the enemy come in. One especially attracted my attention, and he was only about 75 metres off. He moved prettily, and I moved like mad to get out of his sights. But he wasn't my only worry, for there were three or four picking on me alone! No sooner would I avoid one than another one would be firing on me!

Kimber's SPAD S15201 No. 19, which he had christened *Nick III*, was riddled with 70 bullets while he tried to escape in 'a fast, steep right-hand spiral dive, going down almost vertically, and yet turning enough to keep the other fellow's sights off me. For 1200 metres, those streaks and bullets kept flying past me. Then the Boche seemed to pull out of the following dive, evidently convinced that they had sent a SPAD down out of control. I let *Nick* dive vertically for another 800 metres, just for good luck, and then gently pulled him towards our lines'.

In spite of coming under inaccurate anti-aircraft fire during the return flight, Kimber made it back to his aerodrome. 'My landing was terrible and bouncy', he wrote, 'because among other things, the Boche had shot off my left tyre. As I taxied up to the hangars, a great crowd of pilots and mechanics gathered around my aeroplane, and, of course, they had to have the story and congratulate me upon getting away. *Nick* and I were certainly lucky, there's no question about that!'

The 'demise' of Kimber's SPAD was credited to Vzfw Karl Schmückle near St Benoit at 1620 hrs German time for his fifth victory. Five minutes, earlier Ltn von Hantelmann had claimed two SPADs over Lake Lachaussee, one of which was likely S7580 No. 23, which took Phil Hassinger to a fiery death. The other, not confirmed, was flown by 1Lt Robert J. Little, who was driven down in Allied lines unhurt – he subsequently flew his repaired SPAD back to Toul. Ray Brooks' force-landed SPAD S15229 No. 20 *Smith III* was credited to Oblt von Boenigk.

On 26 September Arthur Kimber's luck would run out in a tragically ironic way. Borrowing 1Lt James Beane's SPAD S15268 No. 12 for a strafing mission on the first day of the Meuse-Argonne offensive, Kimber was diving toward the railway station at

Romagne with a payload of four 25lb Cooper bombs when his aeroplane suddenly exploded. An Amercan artillery barrage was going on in the area at that time, and Kimber apparently collided with one of the shells.

In spite of the 'bloody nose' it had suffered on 14 September, the 13th did better the next day, as 1Lt Leighton Brewer noted at the time:

I remember seeing a Fokker, with Hank Stovall's SPAD right behind him, so I tipped up and sprayed right in front of him so that he had to go through my fire, as well as Stovall's. The Fokkers all had red noses and wings, but some of them seemed to have white fuselages, and others had grey.

Hank Stovall and Brewer were credited with a Fokker each, 1Lts Murray Guthrie and Frank K. Hays shared in another and a fourth D VII was credited to Maj Carl A. Spaatz, a staff officer attached to the squadron. 'He said he had three weeks' leave and wanted to spend it getting some practical experience', Brewer recalled. 'He asked to be assigned to the squadron, and be considered as a "Lieutenant" while he was there.' Spaatz would score a second victory on 26 September before leaving the 13th.

With the St Mihiel offensive behind it, the US First Army launched a more ambitious offensive against the German 5. Armee in the Argonne Forest, only to encounter more difficult terrain and a well-entrenched enemy determined to contest every yard. The intensity of the six-week land campaign was matched in the air. The USAS was stronger and its pilots more experienced, but in addition to JG II and the local *Jastas*, they would now be facing JG I 'Richthofen Circus', which arrived in the sector on 26 September – the very day the offensive began.

It was within the first week of the Argonne campaign that SPAD XIII pilots figured in some of the Allied air services' most celebrated exploits. On 25 September, the newly promoted Capt Edward V. Rickenbacker, commander of the 94th Aero Sqn, dived through five Fokker D VIIs to shoot down one of the two LVG reconnaissance aeroplanes that they were escorting, as well as one of the Fokkers. This exploit eventually earned him the Medal of Honor on 6 November 1930.

The 26th saw as much activity on the part of the French as the Americans, most notably the stork-marked SPAD XIIIs of GC12. At 1145 hrs Lt René Fonck of SPA103 drove two Fokker D VIIs down to crash near Sommepy, followed by a Halberstadt two-seater at 1210 hrs. At 1805 hrs Fonck, leading three fellow SPA103 pilots, spotted eight Fokkers over St Souplet. 'I awaited the attack confidently, and would have willingly provoked it when a SPAD came in unexpectedly to lend a hand', he wrote. The interloper was fellow GC12 ace Capt Xavier de Sevin, CO of SPA26.

Fonck claimed that the ensuing fight was one of the most difficult of his career. Adj Jean Brugère downed a Fokker, but was attacked by two others, one of which Fonck claimed in the process of rescuing him. 'During this time', he added, 'Capitaine de Sevin was going through a very risky acrobatic manoeuvre in order to shake off a Boche who had come to grips with him, and who seemed to me to be a rather bold devil. Only the captain's skill as a pilot permitted him to escape, for his motor had conked out and he was pursued to within 100 metres of the ground.'

After a failed balloon attack on 26 September 1918, Vzfw Karl Weinmann's Fokker D VII of Jasta 50 attracts curious Frenchmen at Ville-sur-Tourbe, including Capt Armand de Turenne of SPA12 (left, foreground). He was one of the three pilots from three different *escadrilles* who brought it down. (SHAA B89.1281 via Greg VanWyngarden)

MARK POSTLETHWAITE '08

Five Albatros two-seaters entered the mêlée, and Fonck downed two of them before his machine gun jammed. That raised his day's bag to six. British Sopwith Camel aces John Trollope and Henry Woollett had equalled that feat, but only Fonck had now achieved it twice, having done so previously on 9 May. His success was somewhat marred, however, by de Sevin also claiming one of his Fokkers, only to be robbed of the credit because he had been forced to land, leaving Fonck to submit the sole claim.

De Sevin's SPAD was probably one of two credited to Lt d R Karl Maletzky of Jasta 50. Nearby, however, Vzfw Karl Weinmann tried to attack a French balloon, but he was pounced on by a trio of SPADs from three different *escadrilles*. Brought down and captured, he was jointly credited to SPA12's commander, Capt Armand de Turenne, Adj Emile Régnier of SPA89 and Sous-Lt René Schurck of SPA91.

Finally, on 29 September 2Lt Frank Luke of the 27th Aero Sqn burned three balloons in quick succession before being mortally wounded by ground fire. That morning's exploit brought his tally to 14 balloons and four aircraft, and led to his becoming – posthumously – the first USAS member to receive the Medal of Honor.

On 3 October, Maj J. P. C. Sewell issued a general report on French aviation, which read in part:

The 200hp Hispano-Suiza SPADs are becoming more outclassed every day. Their visibility is bad and their climbing powers insufficient. No new single-seaters seem likely to be turned out in numbers until (at the earliest) the summer of 1919, when SPADs, Nieuports and Dolphins with 300hp Hispano-Suiza engines will probably be in use.

In spite of that pessimistic report, many of the American SPAD XIII pilots were coming fully into their stride in October. Capt Rickenbacker claimed a Fokker D VII that very day, while his squadronmate 1Lt Hamilton Coolidge became an ace by shooting down another D VII and a balloon, then teamed up with Rickenbacker and the 95th Aero Sqn's 1Lt Edwin P. Curtis to destroy an LVG.

While the Americans slogged it out both in and above the Argonne Forest, to their west the French were advancing in the Champagne.

Another of the newer *escadrilles* to enter the struggle was SPA164, formed within GC21 on 13 August around a cadre of pilots from the groupe's SPA124, including its commander, Lt Henri Barancy, and his executive officer, Sous-Lt Marcel Robert. Amongst the new personnel was an American assigned from the USAS, 1Lt Russel C. McCormick.

All of GC21's squadrons were identified by diagonal fuselage bands in different colours, with SPA164's being blue and red. Sous-Lt Robert recalled:

SPA164 was constituted almost entirely of youngsters right out of school. Therefore, we had to perfect their training, teach them how to shoot, drill them in patrol formation flying and familiarise them with the sector. And, until they could be thrown into the fray without too much risk, we had to engage them in warlike activities with prudence.

Weather conditions in September 1918 were particularly bad, and with the end of the war nigh, that explains why we did not have many combats, with some probable but no certain victories. That SPA164 suffered only one loss by the time of the Armistice was a great success in itself.

We had one casualty on 5 September during a fight with a patrol of Fokkers at 4,000 metres over Somme-Py, in the Champagne sector. In the course of that combat, McCormick took a bullet in his leg. For my part, I was busy with four Fokkers, of which three came very close, but without any evident result – at least nothing confirmable.'

Sous-Lt Marcel Robert, deputy commander of SPA164, in a SPAD VII – a less potent but more reliable type whose 180hp version still soldiered on alongside SPAD XIIIs through to the end of the war. (SHAA B87.3855)

Force-landing in Allied lines, the wounded McCormick was posted out of SPA164. He was probably flying the SPAD credited to Ltn Karl Ritscherle of Jasta 60 north of Soissons.

'On 26 September', Robert continued, 'Barancy and I claimed two Fokkers in the region of Assiges, but those were counted only as "probables". On 30 September, Cpls Limay Heine and Gaston Gérain attacked an enemy aeroplane over Challeronge, which fell damaged in enemy lines and could not be confirmed. Heine didn't come back from that patrol, however, and he and his SPAD were found four days later near Cernay wood. That was our only fatality.' Heine may have fallen victim to Vzfw Alfons Nagler of Jasta 81, who claimed a SPAD over Ville that day.

SPA164 was to be credited with only one confirmed victory in its two-and-a-half-month combat career, and Robert was the one who scored it:

On 23 October, I was leading a freelance hunting patrol entirely made up of young pilots when I attacked a two-seat reconnaissance aeroplane at 4,000 metres over Vouziers. The enemy machine caught fire. Too busy watching him fall in flames, I myself was surprised by his escort patrol, which I had not noticed before. My aeroplane was fired on, point-blank, from behind. With my SPAD riddled with bullets, I had to cut my motor, and I tried to glide to our lines – not without pirouetting to evade the volleys of my attackers, who did not leave me alone until we were down to 500 metres. We were then inside French lines, and I was able to land my SPAD without damage in fallow land near a battery zone in the frontline.

German records credited a SPAD in that area to Vzfw Christian Donhauser of Jasta 17, as Robert recalled:

Yes, it's certainly I who was confirmed to Vzfw Donhauser, even though he hadn't 'shot me down' in the strict sense of the term, but only forced me to land near Vrizy, under his eyes but without the slightest damage, in our lines in a large field of stubble. I then took off from here again two hours later after a fortunate repair allowed me to return my motor to working order. Since then, I have never understood why he didn't finish me while I was stopped on the ground. Doubtless he was afraid of the fire of the anti-aircraft artillery batteries near which I had landed.

At 1610 hrs on 29 October, 1Lt James Beane led his flight down on eight low-flying Fokkers over Aincreville. In the ensuing fight, he was credited with one in flames and a second shared with 1Lt Remington deB. Vernam – bringing both of their scores to six – while 1Lts Jacques M. Swaab and Clinton Jones claimed a third Fokker. Their

Ltn Christian Donhauser of Jasta 17, seen here with a Fokker D VII (F) at Colbenz in January 1919, was credited with shooting down Sous-Lt Robert on 23 October 1918, but the Frenchman survived to land in Allied lines. He duly repaired his engine and flew back to Somme-Vesle two hours later.
(Greg VanWyngarden)

ENGAGING THE ENEMY

By the time SPAD XIIIs encountered Fokker D VIIs in the spring of 1918, fighter pilots on both sides had a choice of gunsights. The earliest and simplest involved lining up a bead on a pylon with a ring about three inches in diameter, with four radial wires attached to an inner ring of 0.5- and 1-inch diameter, which allowed for the speed and direction of a moving target, as well as that of the pilot's own aeroplane.

A more sophisticated option was developed by the Aldis brothers of Sparkhill, Birmingham, in 1915. They constructed a tube that contained a series of lenses marked with two concentric rings that transmitted parallel light rays, its centre always being directly on the axis of the sight regardless of the position of the aimer's eye. Both the Aldis sight and its French equivalent, the Collimateur Crétien, were hermetically sealed to contain an inert gas, which prevented the lenses from fogging. The German Oigee firm's version was said to lack the inert gas, which limited its usefulness.

A few pilots eschewed both systems. 'I replaced the Aldis with a triple bead and "V" sight of my own invention', said André Martenot de Cordoux of SPA94, 'lining up my target with a set of cross hairs without glass nearest to my eye, a bead midway down the gun, and a "V" aperture near the muzzle.'

'I used a Ray-Soulte sight', said Leighton Brewer of the 13th Aero Sqn. 'Hank Stovall and I were the only ones that did – I didn't like looking through all the metal of the other kind. The Ray-Soulte

was just two little red beads, mounted at the opposite ends of a bar, and you lined up your target between them. Sort of automatically computed the right lead if it was lined up right.'

Whichever sight one used, in a dogfight a pilot had to avoid becoming fixated on a target for more than a few seconds, since it narrowed his peripheral vision. The consequences were best summed up by an American adage that has applied to aerial combat ever since – 'It's the one you don't see that gets you.'

Depicted here is the death of Offstv Otto Esswein of Jasta 26, who had been credited with 12 victories, mostly in Fokker Dr Is, by 31 May 1918. Before fully coming into his stride in the new D VII, he was shot down near Hartennes on 21 July. The ace had fallen victim either to Sous-Lt Maurice Boyau of SPA77, who was credited with an enemy aeroplane in flames south of Soissons at 1905 hrs for his 25th victory, or Lt Henri Hay de Slade of SPA86, who specified a D VII in flames southeast of Belleu at 1745 hrs for his 11th.

opponents were probably from Jasta 6, which claimed two SPADs – whose pilots, 1Lts John C. Crissey and Frank B. Tyndall, actually landed safely in Allied lines – while suffering the loss of Lt d R Martin Fischer, killed near Montfaucon, south of Aincreville.

On 4 November the 103rd Aero Sqn's B Flight was in action again, as recounted by DeFreest Larner:

My B Flight reached its peak during this action. We were on patrol when I spotted a *Staffel* of seven Fokkers, and I quickly led my flight into a favourable position between them and the sun. All this time, the Germans gave no indication that they had seen us – they could not have been a very experienced outfit. When all was ready, down we went, and we stayed above the Fokkers throughout the fight that followed. We shot or drove all seven of them down, of which three were officially credited – one to 1Lt John Frost, one to 1Lt Herbert B. Bartholf and I, and one to me alone. The final success of this mission was also the 32nd, and last, victory for the 103rd Aero Sqn since it had officially joined the American Expeditionary Forces (AEF) in July 1918. Not one of us had been touched.

The previous day, with the Germans falling back on all fronts, JG I's adjutant, Oblt Karl Bodenschatz, recorded eight victories in the *Geschwader* log, and commented on the general situation:

Now there is practically no rest. The American offensive on the ground continues without interruption. Behind shot-up waves come more waves, and behind these come more and more, and still more!

And in the air, when enemy squadrons retreat, fresh squadrons take their place again and again and again! When the aeroplanes of the Richthofen Geschwader land, the pilots do not even give a thought to the bullet holes in their wings. They return from every combat mission with a greater wonder than it was before possible that they had survived and returned once more.

The next day JG I tallied four more victories, and noted, 'The men turn their backs on rumours, put on their fur-lined boots and climb behind their machine guns. Nothing else matters.'

On 6 November the 28th Aero Sqn got an indication of the state of German fighter pilot morale as the war came to an end. 1Lt Martinus Stenseth shared his eighth victory with 1st Lts Hugh C. McClung and Ben E. Brown when they shot down a two-seater over the Forêt de Woevre. McClung, however, was injured when engine failure caused him to crash-land near Bethelainville. Meanwhile, Brown was attacked by Fokkers of Jasta 6, wounded and brought down in German lines. He was the 30th, and last, victory for Ltn Ulrich Neckel, and for JG I. Brown reported:

The four Fokker pilots who chased me down came to Loupy le Château to shake hands with me. Ltn Neckel was their flight commander. He told me who he was and then complimented me for getting the bi-place. They seemed to be a very sporty lot of pilots.

STATISTICS AND ANALYSIS

Any attempt at trying to accurately compare the performance of the SPAD XIII when in combat with the Fokker D VII is handicapped by several factors, starting with the difficulty in ascertaining the aircraft type being described in each side's combat reports. In the second half of 1918 the French had a tendency to refer to all their fighter opposition as either an *'avion de chasse'* or a 'Fokker', which by that late stage of the war had become synonymous terms to them – as indeed it had earlier, in reference to Eindeckers during the 'Fokker Scourge' of 1915–16.

Even when the odd French or American claim specified that the aircraft destroyed was a 'Fokker D VII', one still cannot be 100 percent sure whether or not the victim might in fact have been a Pfalz D XII. Indeed, the latter type's car-type radiator and N-shaped struts gave it a superficial similarity to its more famous stablemate at a distance or in the heat of combat.

The Germans, on the other hand, often referred generically to SPADs, which even late in the war could just as likely refer to the 180hp SPAD VII as to the XIII, since many French *escadrilles* – unlike the exclusively SPAD XIII-equipped USAS aero squadrons – were still flying both types. For that matter, their references to 'SPADs' could often extend to SPAD XI or XVI two-seaters, or misidentified Salmson 2A2s.

Another problem lies with the already common phenomenon of overclaiming. One usually prefers to attribute the discrepancies between pilot and squadron tallies against records of actual enemy losses to over-optimistic misperceptions of the extent of the damage done to the enemy aeroplane, multiple claims on the same victim or plain wishful thinking, but in all cases made in good faith.

French infantrymen examine the remains of Cpl Limay Heine's SPAD XIII of SPA164. Heine was killed near Challerange on 30 September 1918, having probably fallen victim to Vzfw Alfons Nagler of Jasta 81. (SHAA B87.3888)

Verification was generally easier for the Germans than for the Allies because the fighting occurred more over their territory. However, a closer look at their claims compared to some of the more detailed Allied squadron or personal logs reveals numerous instances of French or American SPADs credited to German pilots that in fact force-landed on the Allied side of the lines, with the pilot slightly injured or unhurt and the damage to the aeroplane itself often quickly repairable. In September 1918, for example, German fighter pilots were credited with a total of 147 'SPADs', whereas the French listed 42 SPAD XIIIs and the Americans 37 lost during the course of the month. Even allowing for two-seaters among the German claims, it is clear that their perceptions could be just as faulty as those of their opponents, even with the advantage of fighting more often over their own side of the lines.

Accounts by Allied pilots of how they were brought down, but nevertheless survived their run-ins with the enemy, do much to explain how the French or Americans may have been credited to Fokker units when no corresponding dead, wounded or PoWs appear on the German casualty lists. Fighting behind his own lines, a German pilot had a better chance of force-landing a damaged or disabled aeroplane safely – and if all else failed, he could keep off the 1918 casualty list by taking to his parachute, provided it worked.

Given the similar performance of their fighters, the SPAD and Fokker pilots faced differing challenges toward attaining or maintaining air superiority in the last months of the war. Tactically, the Germans derived much benefit from usually fighting over their home ground with the prevailing wind blowing their way. Thus, a downed Fokker and its pilot – unless he was killed – both faced better odds of being recovered and returned to combat.

The pilot of a damaged or disabled SPAD, on the other hand, faced a difficult flight or glide back to his lines. A remarkable number of SPAD pilots did make it back, partly through skill and determination, and in no small measure thanks to the robust construction of their aeroplanes.

All other factors being equal, a battle of attrition favoured the Germans. However, all factors were not equal, as the Allies had the numbers, and unrestricted access to fuel and ammunition, to retain the initiative in spite of their losses. And they did inflict casualties on the Germans, which the latter were less able to afford.

One way of gauging a fighter's success can lie in comparing the outcomes when the best pilots flying the rival types met. Known SPAD XIII aces who fell victim to Fokker D VIIs included no fewer than three aces who died at the hands of the same German pilot within a week – David E. Putnam (13 victories), Maurice Boyau (35 victories) and Joseph F. Wehner (five victories), all credited to Georg von Hantelmann. In addition, on 16 July 1918 Sous-Lt André Barcat of SPA153 (five victories) was killed, along with squadronmate Sous-Lt Georges Lutzius, in the Suippes area by Ltn Hans Pippart and Vzfw Richard Schneider of Jasta 19.

On 10 October, one day after scoring his fifth victory and being promoted to lieutenant, Russian volunteer Viktor Federov of SPA89 was wounded in a SPAD XIII, possibly by Ltn Max Näther of Jasta 62. On the same day, 2Lt Wilbert W. White of the 147th Aero Sqn was killed in a head-on collision with a Fokker, and was posthumously credited with it as his eighth victory. The German pilot, Ltn Walter Kohlbach of Jasta 10, survived thanks to his parachute and was credited with White's SPAD for his fifth, and final, victory. Kohlbach was also claimed by – and credited to – Capt Rickenbacker!

1Lt Karl Schoen Jr of the 139th Aero Sqn shared in the destruction of two Fokkers over Damvillers at 1520 hrs on 29 October, taking his score to seven, just before he too was shot down and killed, probably by Ltn Friedrich Schliewen of Jasta 6. Two aces of the 22nd Aero Sqn fell victim to Fokkers on 30 October, 1Lt James D. Beane (six victories) being killed and 1Lt Remington deB. Vernam (five victories) taken prisoner and subsequently dying of his wounds.

Known Fokker D VII losses to SPAD XIIIs began with Offstv Otto Esswein, a successful Dr I ace of Jasta 26 who added little or nothing to his 12 victories in his new D VII before being killed on 21 July 1918, probably by Sous-Lt Boyau of SPA77. Four days later Ltn Karl Menckhoff, CO of Jasta 72s and victor over 39 Allied aeroplanes, suffered the humiliation of being brought down and captured following combat with 1Lt Walter L. Avery, a relative neophyte in the American 95th Aero Sqn.

On 3 October Ltn Fritz Höhn, CO of Jasta 41 with 21 victories, was mortally wounded over St Martin l'Heureux, either by Sous-Lt André Martenot de Cordoux

This Fokker D VII in 1st Pursuit Group hands at Rembercourt aerodrome is believed to have been the aircraft flown by Ltn Gustav Böhren of Jasta 10 that was brought down near Exermont on 18 October 1918 by 1Lt Albert J. Weatherhead Jr of the 95th Aero Sqn. (Greg VanWyngarden)

of SPA94, who claimed a probable D VII there, or Lt Robert Le Petit of SPA67, who was credited with a D VII over Dontrien, just south of St Martin. On 23 October Vzfw Gustav Klaudat of Jasta 15 (six victories) was wounded and put out of the war by Capt Edward V. Rickenbacker, CO of the 94th Aero Sqn. On the 27th, Vzfw Karl Paul Schlegel, a 22-victory ace of Jasta 45, was killed by Sous-Lt Pierre Marinovitch of SPA94.

One possible additional SPAD-credited German casualty was Ltn Oliver von Beaulieu-Marconnay, CO and 25-victory ace of Jasta 19. On 18 October he was attacking a SPAD when he was wounded in the thigh, and although he made it back to his aerodrome, he died of post-operative complications on the 26th, just after receiving the *Orden Pour le Mérite*. Several D VII claims were made that day, including one near Landre by 1Lt Chester E. Wright of the 93rd Aero Sqn that Lt Louis Risacher of SPA159 testified to be one of several Fokkers that were attacking him – he claimed to have subsequently turned on his assailants and downed another D VII over Buzançy. The Germans, however, determined that Beaulieu had in fact been hit by a German bullet, possibly fired amid the confusion of battle by a member of Jasta 74.

Adding up the claims yields a total of nine SPAD aces killed, wounded or captured by Fokkers, against six D VII masters whose losses were credited in one way or another to SPAD pilots if one gives von Beaulieu-Marconnay's case the benefit of the doubt. It should be noted, however, that for every casualty there was an ace credited to his enemies who lived to fight another day.

American World War I ace of aces, commander of the 94th Aero Sqn and victor over a record (for SPAD pilots) 12 Fokker D VIIs, Capt Edward V. Rickenbacker strikes a classic pose beside SPAD XIII S4523 'Old Number 1' at Rembercourt aerodrome in October 1918. (Greg VanWyngarden)

On the Allied side, 1Lt Sumner Sewell was apparently shot down in flames by Hptm Oskar *Freiherr* von Boenigk, CO of JG II, but survived miraculously unhurt. Von Boenigk may also have claimed 1Lt Arthur Raymond Brooks' SPAD the next day, although Brooks, credited with his fourth and fifth victories in that same melée, survived to score a sixth before the armistice.

On 26 September Lt Xavier de Sevin, 12-victory ace and CO of SPA26, was brought down in French lines and probably credited to Ltn de R Karl Maletsky of Jasta 50. De Sevin was unhurt, however. A more grievous loss to SPA26 occurred on 5 October when Lt Roland Garros was lost. A pioneer of fighter aviation's earliest days, who had been captured by the Germans in April 1915, escaped, returned to combat and brought his tally to near-acedome at four, Garros was killed by Ltn de R Hermann Habich of Jasta 49.

Besides the mutual credits logged for White and Kohlbach, Ltns Justus Grassmann and Aloys Heldmann were credited with SPADs on 10 October, which American records would suggest correspond to the death of 2Lt William E. Brotherton of the 147th Aero Sqn and to Brotherton's CO, Capt James A. Meissner. Although the latter pilot's SPAD was shot

Oblt Oskar Freiherr von Boenigk commanded JG II from mid-August 1918 through to the end of the war, inflicting heavy casualties on the Americans and increasing his own score to 26 (eight of which were SPAD XIIIs). (Greg VanWyngarden)

up, Meissner actually made it back to base at Rembercourt unharmed and survived the war with eight victories.

On the German side, Ltn Näther of Jasta 62 was slightly wounded on 27 September, and was possibly credited to 1Lt William J. Hoover of the 27th Aero Sqn. Back in action on 23 October, Näther duly burned a balloon and was subsequently attacked, claimed by and credited to 1Lt Jacques M. Swaab of the 22nd Aero Sqn, although this time he evidently survived uninjured.

The latter date also saw Ltn Friedrich Noltenius of Jasta 11 burn a 'gasbag' of the American 2nd Balloon Company and then come under attack from some vindictive SPADs. 'I applied full throttle and escaped at the double-double quick', Noltenius wrote in his diary. 'The SPADs did not react with sufficient determination, and shot at me from behind at very long range, so I escaped unscathed.' One of his assailants, 1Lts Lansing C. Holden of the 95th Aero Sqn, admitted in a letter that 'It was a stern chase, and he got away', yet the AEF credited him and his partner, 1Lt Edwin P. Curtis, with shooting Noltenius' Fokker down!

The overall toll taken on Allied aircraft of all types by Fokker D VIIs in the war's final months was indisputably heavy. As far as their performance against SPAD XIIIs goes, however, the conclusion that emerges from a careful analysis of claims and losses on both sides proves to be curiously inconclusive.

Leading SPAD XIII Fokker D VII Killers

French Pilots	Squadron(s)	D VIIs	Total
Capt René Paul Fonck	SPA103	9	75
Lt Bernard H. Barny de Romanet	SPA37 & 167	7	18
Lt Georges Félix Madon	SPA38	6	41
American Pilots	**Squadron**	**D VIIs**	**Total**
Capt Edward V. Rickenbacker	94th AS	12	26
1Lt Frank O'D. Hunter	103rd AS	7	9
1Lt Murray K. Guthrie	13th AS	6	6
1Lt Frank K. Hays	13th AS	6	6
1Lt Leslie J. Rummell	93rd AS	6	7
1Lt Chester E. Wright	93rd AS	6	9
1Lt James D. Beane	22nd AS	5	6
Capt Reed McK. Chambers	94th AS	5	7
1Lt Charles R. D'Olive	93rd AS	5	5
1Lt Harold H. George	139th AS	5	5
Capt Martinus. Stenseth	28th AS	5	8
Capt Jacques M. Swaab	22nd AS	5	10

Leading Fokker D VII SPAD XIII Killers

Pilot	Jasta(s)	SPAD XIIIs	Total
Ltn Georg von Hantelmann	15	15	25
Ltn Erich Löwenhardt	10	14	53
Ltn Franz Büchner	13	13	40
Ltn Hans Christian F. Donhauser	27	10	19
Ltn Walter Blume	9	9	28
Ltn Arthur Laumann	66 & 10	9	28
Ltn Max Näther	62	9	26
Ltn Ernst Udet	4	8	62
Oblt Oskar *Freiherr* von Boenigk	21 & JG II	8	26
Ltn Gustav Dörr	45	6	35
Ltn Oliver von Beaulieu-Marconnay	15 & 19	6	25
Ltn Alois Heldmann	10	6	15
Ltn Carl Menckhoff	72s	5	39
Ltn Ulrich Neckel	12, 19 & 6	5	30
Ltn Hermann Becker	12	5	23
Ltn Hans Müller	18	5	12
Ltn Richard Wenzl	6	5	12
Vzfw Alfons Nagler	81	5	10

AFTERMATH

There were 1,069 Fokker D VIIs at the front at the time of the armistice, with 78 *Jagdstaffeln* having anywhere from six to 12 of them on strength. A grand total of 2,768 were eventually delivered. In contrast, no fewer than 8,472 SPAD XIIIs were produced by nine contractors, of which 893 had been delivered to the USAS by the time the war came to an end.

Although the German Army was collapsing all over the front from Flanders to Lorraine, the beleaguered *Jagdstaffeln* remained full of fight up until they got their orders to stand down. Many of the fighter pilots accepted news of the Kaiser's abdication and their country's capitulation with a combination of incredulity and disgust that in many cases lent itself to later acceptance of the Nazi-encouraged myth of a German Army stabbed in the back by profiteers, communists and traitors, predominantly Jewish.

The hard fact, however, is that the *Jagdflieger's* war was all but lost before their world-beating Fokker D VIIs were available in anywhere near the numbers required to make a difference. There had been just 19 examples of the fighter at the front on 1 May 1918, by which point the British had recovered from the first shock of Operation *Michael* – and the Luftstreitskräfte's most inspirational ace, and fighter leader, Manfred von Richthofen, was already dead. By 1 July, when 407 Fokker D VIIs were operational, the Third Battle of the Aisne (27 May to 3 June) and the advances on Noyon and Montdidier (9–13 June) had ended with the French Army firmly holding, and showing no sign of collapse. On 1 September, when 838 Fokkers were at the front, the French, British and Americans were all either on, or about to go on, the offensive.

The SPAD XIII continued a postwar career for years, being phased out of frontline French service by newer types in 1923. American SPAD XIIIs, re-engined with 180hp

Postwar casualty. While taking off in SPAD XIII S18867 on 21 December 1918, Capt Hobart A. H. 'Hobey' Baker, commander of the 141st Aero Sqn and a 103rd Aero Sqn veteran with two victories to his credit, crashed to his death. (Greg VanWyngarden)

Wright-Hispano Es, were used as fighter trainers. SPAD XIIIs also saw postwar service with the air forces of Belgium, Poland, Czechoslovakia, Portugal, Spain, Thailand and Japan.

So impressed were the Allies by the Fokker D VII's performance that the Treaty of Versailles included a specific demand for the surrender of 1,700 of the fighters. Ironically, in order to meet those terms the Germans had to continue production into 1919! After the 142 D VIIs ceded to the United States underwent flight evaluation, many were pressed into service with the US Army Air Service, US Navy and

A Fokker D VII surrendered to US forces after the armistice undergoes evaluation at McCook Field, Ohio. (Jon Guttman)

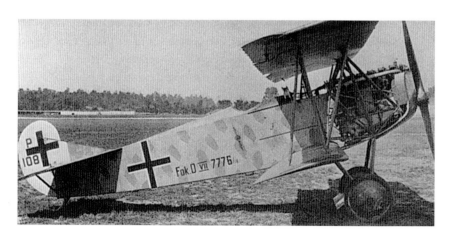

US Marine Corps, influencing subsequent American biplane fighter designs. Others found their way to Hollywood, where they were used – and, all too often, used up in deliberately staged crashes – in such films as *Hell's Angels*.

Never one to let a treaty stand in the way of business, Anthony Fokker managed to smuggle 400 engines and parts to 120 aircraft out of Germany so he could tool up for resumed production in his native Holland, where the D VII and its two-seater derivative, the C I, became mainstays and the progenitors of further generations of Dutch biplanes whose service extended to World War II.

As late as 1929, the Swiss Alfred Comte firm built eight D VIIs under licence to supplement the interned specimens serving in the Fliegertruppe. Belgium, which received 324 Fokkers, used them until 1931. Fokker D VIIs also saw postwar service with the air arms of Poland, Czechoslovakia, Finland, Lithuania, Sweden, Rumania, Latvia and the Soviet Union. Not bad for an aeroplane whose use was supposedly controlled by the Treaty of Versailles.

Fokker D VII 4635/18 of Jasta 65, which had landed at the 1st Pursuit Group's advance field at Verdun on 9 November 1918 – in error according to its pilot, Ltn Heinz von Beaulieu-Marconnay – shows a wealth of detail as it undergoes restoration at the Smithsonian Institution in Washington, DC. (Greg VanWyngarden)

FURTHER READING

BOOKS

Biddle, Maj C. J., *Fighting Airman: The Way of the Eagle* (Ace Books, 1968)

Bruce, J. M., *SPAD 13.C1* (Windsock Datafile 32, Albatross Productions, 1992)

Fonck, Capt R., edited by Stanley M. Ulanoff, *Ace of Aces* (Doubleday & Co., 1967)

Franks, N. L. R., Bailey, F. W. and Guest, R., *Above the Lines* (Grub Street, 1993)

Franks, N. L. R. and Bailey, F. W., *Over the Front* (Grub Street, 1992)

Franks, N. L. R. and Bailey, F. W., *The Storks* (Grub Street, London)

La Vie Aérienne Illustrée, 1917-18

Gray, P. L., *The Fokker D VII* (Profile Publications, Ltd No 25)

Kilduff, P., *The Red Baron Combat Wing: Jagdgeschwader Richthofen in Battle* (Arms & Armour Press, 1997)

Porret, D., *Les "As" français de la Grande Guerre* (Service Historique de l'Armée de l'Air, Château de Vincennes, 1983)

Rickenbacker, E. V., *Fighting the Flying Circus* (Avon Books, 1965)

Wenzl, R., *Richthofen-Flieger* (Freiburg im Breisgau, 1930)

MAGAZINES

Abbott, D-S., 'The Fokker D VII in Service', *Over the Front* (Fall 2000)

Duiven, R., 'Das Königliches Jagdgeschwader Nr.II', *Over the Front* (Fall 1994)

Bailey, F. W., 'The 103rd Aero, USAS (Formerly Lafayette Escadrille)', *Cross & Cockade (USA) Journal* (Winter 1978)

Brewer, L., 'How It Was', *Cross & Cockade (USA) Journal* (Spring 1962)

Bruce, J. M., 'SPAD Story', *Air International* (May 1976)

Guttman, J., 'The Hard-Luck Escadrille: Markings and a Short History of SPA159 *'Le Poing'*, *Over the Front* (Summer 1988)

Guttman, J., 'Triumphs and Tribulations: Pierre de Cazenove de Pradines', *Cross & Cockade (USA) Journal* (Spring 1980)

Jeanes, W., 'The Diary of Captain Richard Denny Shelvy, DSC', *Over the Front* (Summer 2007)

Täger, H., 'A Man for Sonderfilme: Rudolf Windisch', *Over the Front* (Fall 2002)

INDEX